One
Love,
One
Heart

One Love, One Heart

A HISTORY OF REGGAE

JAMES HASKINS

JUMP AT THE SUN

HYPERION BOOKS FOR CHILDREN

NEW YORK

First Edition
1 3 5 7 9 10 8 6 4 2

Printed in the United States of America
Library of Congress Cataloging-in-Publication Data
on file.

ISBN 0-7868-0479-3

Visit www.jumpatthesun.com

Photo credits can be found on page 134.

CONTENTS

One
Love,
One
Heart

PREFACE: REGGAE RHYTHMS

Caribbean Sea

JAMAICA

Jamaica Channel

KINGSTON
★

Caribbean Sea

REGGAE IS JAMAICA'S QUINTESSENTIAL MUSIC.
Reggae has its roots in the folk music of the island;
in the drumming of African slaves brought by white
settlers to work the land; in mento, Jamaica's own
version of calypso, played by rural musicians; and in
American and Jamaican popular music of the 1940s,
'50s, and '60s—New Orleans rhythm and blues, ska,
and rock steady. Reggae is equally rooted in the hope
instilled by the Rastafarian religion, and in the harsh
life of the island's urban poor.

A reggae song has three simple ingredients, the bass line, the tune, and the lyrics, which combine to produce an offbeat bounce. The highly melodic bass line forms a foundation over which the tune is played and the lyrics are sung or chanted. Early reggae songs were often humorous, like the traditional mento songs, but as social and political unrest fermented in the ghettos of Kingston and other cities in Jamaica, the lyrics began to reflect this, and were used as a vehicle to convey the message of the Rastafarian religion prominent in the ghetto. What eventually emerged was what has come to be called "roots reggae," a music of the people.

Reggae has become synonymous with Jamaica. It has had an enormous influence on such popular musicians as Eric Clapton, Cat Stevens, and Paul Simon, and on American rappers of the 1990s and beyond, and its popularity continues today. It is a music that captures the universal, timeless desires for peace and a better world. Because these hopes never die, reggae rhythms continue to thrive.

1
SWEET JAMAICA

Sun is shining, the weather is sweet
Make you want to move your dancing feet

—"Sun is Shining," Bob Marley[1]

A LITTLE MORE THAN 500 MILES SOUTH-SOUTHEAST of Miami, Florida, the island of Jamaica basks in the tropical sun. Just 146 miles long and 50 miles wide, the island is home to a people whose ancestors came from many different countries, hence its official motto: "Out of many, one people." With its blue skies, soft winds, alluring white-sand beaches, and thickly forested mountains graced by sparkling waterfalls, the island has drawn travelers since early times. Around A.D. 650, the Arawak Indians, also called the Taíno, a people who came from South America, were lured to the shores of Jamaica in their canoes made from hollowed-out tree trunks. Naming their new home "Xaymaca," meaning "land of springs," the Arawak settled in small farming and fishing communities.

The gentle Arawak flourished in their new home, and to them it must have seemed like paradise. This paradise, however, ended on May 4, 1494, when Christopher Columbus landed on the island during his second voyage to the West Indies. Perhaps the Arawak had some presentiment of their fate because, although ordinarily a peaceful people, they attacked Columbus's ships when he tried to come ashore at what is now St. Ann's Bay on the island's north coast. Driven off but determined, Columbus finally landed the next day at what is now known as Discovery Bay, claiming the island for Spain and naming it St. Iago.

The Spanish sought in Jamaica what they sought elsewhere in the New World: gold. Starting around 1510, they established their first settlements to seek this precious metal. The first settlement, Sevilla la Nueva (New Seville), was built near St. Ann's Bay, and others soon followed, including Villa de la Vega (later simply called Spanish Town), which became the capital of the island until 1872, when the government shifted to Kingston. Although the Arawak had some gold ornaments acquired through trade with other islands and along the coast of South

America, the Spanish search for gold in great quantities was fruitless. Lacking the lure of gold, the rulers in Spain lost much of their interest in the island, and carved it up into land grants to be given as favors to members of the Spanish nobility. These nobles established plantations, hewn out of the tropical forest for them by the Arawak, that were devoted to growing sugarcane, citrus, cocoa, bananas, and other crops that could be exported to Spain and other parts of the world.

The Arawak were forced to labor as slaves for their new Spanish rulers. Within a short time, their violent mistreatment and European diseases, to which the Arawak had no resistance, led to the Indians' extinction. Many simply committed suicide in the face of the intolerable labor and the cruelty of the Spanish, hanging themselves or drinking the poisonous juice of the cassava that grows on the island. Since the Arawak had no written language, the fact that they existed at all is marked only by the presence of a few artifacts and cave paintings that have survived to the present day. With the death of the Arawak, the Spanish needed workers to replace them, so they began importing slaves from West Africa in 1517. These new slaves were put to work as field hands tilling the soil to grow crops for export, and as servants in the breezy homes of their Spanish masters.

Because there was no gold, Spain had little interest in maintaining control of the island; the colonists
were left to loosely govern and to defend themselves. The British, however, did have an interest in
the island, and in 1655, Lord Protector Oliver
Cromwell instructed Admiral William Penn of the
British navy to lead an expeditionary fleet to
Jamaica. The fleet reached the island in May of that
year, invaded with 8,000 troops, and seized control
of the island from the Spanish colonists. Rather than
fight a losing battle, the colonists fled north to Cuba
or back to Spain, leaving the island to Penn and his
troops. Before fleeing, though, the colonists freed
and armed their many slaves, instructing them to
harass the British until the colonists could return to
reclaim their land.

The newly freed slaves escaped to the remote
mountains of Jamaica where, earlier, small communities had been established by runaway slaves. Because
the mountains were largely inaccessible, the runaways
had remained well hidden from their masters, as did,
now, those slaves freed by the fleeing Spanish. "These
were the earliest Maroons [from the Spanish word
cimarron, meaning "wild" or "living on peaks"], the
first in a long line of independent-minded black
Jamaicans, whose ranks were expanded in successive
years by other runaways."[2] The Maroons made con-
tinual raids upon the British, harassing them with

Workers carry heavy loads on a plantation in Jamaica.

guerrilla tactics, not because they had been instructed to do so by their former Spanish masters, but because they were determined to retain their independence.

After the Spanish colonists fled Jamaica, Spain engaged in numerous, albeit halfhearted, forays against the British and against British ships in an attempt to regain control of the island. Finally, in 1670, the Treaty of Madrid formally ceded control of Jamaica to the British, ending the period of conflict.

Before the signing of the Treaty of Madrid, however, Jamaica had begun to flourish under British rule. Along with a lucrative slave trade, crops grown on the island were sent back to England and exported to Europe, bringing wealth to the new plantation owners. There was, additionally, another, less legal source of wealth flowing into the country from a group called "buccaneers."

Buccaneers "had originally been a motley crew of renegades who hunted pigs and cattle in the north of Hispaniola, and traded with passing ships. Their name comes from *boucan*, the wooden frame on which they cured th[eir] meat."[3] The buccaneers may have begun as traders, but because of their hatred of Spanish rule, they took to their own ships and quickly graduated to seizing the wealth and arms of passing Spanish ships, encouraged by the British and the French, who also sought a foothold in the West Indies.

Port Royal in Kingston Harbor became the buccaneers' port of choice and was soon transformed into a rowdy, rough, cutthroat town. Buccaneers, privateers (mercenary seamen hired by one country to attack another's merchant fleet), and pirates caroused, fought, and spent their ill-gotten gains in the taverns and brothels of the town. For the right amount of gold, anything or anyone could be bought in Port Royal. In 1664, the British governor of Jamaica, Thomas Modyford, attempted to clean up Port Royal, using British troops to kick the buccaneers out of town. Many of them traveled on to the island of Tortuga off the coast of Haiti to find their fun, but others used the occasion to retire from the roving, seafaring life, settling in Jamaica and establishing farms or running taverns and other businesses.

Despite their attempts to rid the island of this disreputable element, in 1670 the British found themselves having to call upon the buccaneers for aid. Spanish attacks on British ships had become more frequent and fierce. The British asked a former buccaneer, Henry Morgan, leader of the Brethren of the Coast, to come out of retirement to fend off the Spanish. Named "Admiral and Commander-in-Chief of all the ships of war belonging to this harbor [Kingston]," Morgan and his men began a series of forays against the Spanish, culminating in a triumphant raid on Panama City in 1671 that ended with their burning the city to the ground.

Because the raid took place after the Treaty of Madrid had been signed, the Spanish lodged a formal complaint with the British that could not be ignored if further relations between the two countries were to be friendly. Jamaican governor Thomas Modyford and various buccaneers were arrested and transported to England for trial. Despite the fact that Modyford and the buccaneers claimed not to have received word of the signing of the Treaty of Madrid until after the raid on Panama City, Modyford was sentenced to prison in England, but was quickly pardoned. The next year, Henry Morgan was called to England and tried for piracy. He was acquitted, then knighted for his service to the crown. Morgan returned to Jamaica in triumph as lieutenant governor of the island; soon thereafter, he was appointed governor.

Ironically, during his term as governor, Morgan tried to crack down on the carousing in Port Royal of the very buccaneers with whom he had earlier con-sorted, jailing many of them during his term in office. It took Mother Nature herself to finally do away with the evils of Port Royal, however. On June 7, 1692, the town was leveled by an earthquake and by the fires that followed, and nearly 2,000 of its 8,000 residents were killed. Those surviving relocated to Kingston and other parts of Jamaica, formally ending the colorful era of the buccaneer. Later, Port Royal became an important British naval station.

Although the farms and plantations of Jamaica grew a variety of crops, sugar was increasingly becom-ing the island's dominant export. In 1673, there had been 57 sugar plantations; by 1737, there were 430. But growing sugar demanded a huge labor force. During the eighteenth century, more and more slaves were imported from Africa for this purpose. "By 1800 there were 300,000 slaves to work the plantation, 15 times the number of whites on the island."[4] The slave trade thrived as one point of the triangle trade system of the 1700s. Jamaica exported rum and other goods to England and Europe. With part of the profits, traders bought slaves in Africa who were taken either to Jamaica and other Caribbean colonies to work on the plantations, or transported along with Jamaican sugar and rum to America to be sold to toil in the fields of the southern American colonies. Slave labor and the slave trade made Jamaica the wealthiest of the Caribbean islands, but at a tremendous cost in human suffering. Jamaica's wealth was concentrated in the hands of a small minority of the island's population, the white planters and shipping magnates.

Most of the Africans kidnapped into slavery came from the Gold and Ivory Coasts and Benin, where the Coromantee, Ibo, and Mandingo tribes, among others, lived. Uprooted from their homes, torn from their families, they were loaded like cattle onto ships and transported to Jamaica and other places in the New World to be sold. Those slaves who lived on the island endured horrific conditions caused by not only the backbreaking work in the fields growing sugar, but by the dangers of refining it. Before any sort of mechanized process for refining sugar had been developed, slaves had to tend the fires and handle the huge cauldrons of boiling sugar by hand. Many were badly burned and even killed making sugar for the rest of the world.

The slaves were ruled with an iron hand by their European overseers, who greatly feared the possibility of rebellion. Slaves far outnumbered their owners, and rebellion was a very real threat. In 1760, for example, a slave named Tacky led a rebellion in the area of Port Maria on the north coast of Jamaica. Although it was quickly put down, Tacky's Rebellion ignited a number of other, smaller revolts. These, too, were brutally stamped out. In the wake of these revolts, the planters tightened their control over their slaves, making the slaves' conditions even more harsh.

Some slaves did manage to escape their brutal servitude, however. Those who did fled to join the Maroons in the highlands. There they were able to live a relatively free existence, scraping a living from the soil and only descending from the mountains to harass the British landowners. The British fought a running battle with the Maroons for nearly fifty years. Finally, in 1739, the British signed a peace treaty with the Maroons. The treaty granted the Maroons freedom on their own land over which neither the planters nor the colonial governors were to have jurisdiction. In return, though, the Maroons were to aid the British in capturing any further runaway slaves and rebels.

In 1807, Great Britain abolished slavery. Jamaican slaveholders, however, resisted freeing their slaves. Not only were slaves necessary to sugar growing and production, but the plantation owners feared what the slaves might do if freed, since they far outnumbered the white population on the island. "In 1775, for example, Jamaica was inhabited by 13,000 whites and more than 200,000 blacks, virtually all of them slaves. Today only 4 percent of Jamaica's population of slightly more than 2.5 million people is white, while 91 percent is black or of black ancestry."[5]

In 1831, a rebellion led by "Daddy" Sam Sharpe, a Baptist preacher, forced the government to start to take the steps that would lead at last to the end of slavery. Although Sharpe was hanged for his role in the rebellion—the square in Montego Bay where he was hanged is now named for him—the fate of slavery in Jamaica was sealed, and, in 1838, the British Parliament emancipated the island's slaves.

With the emancipation of Jamaica's slaves, sugar production—and the overall wealth of the island—began to decline. Most of the newly freed blacks refused to work for wages in the sugar fields where they had suffered under the harsh eye and whip of the overseer, choosing instead to work their own, meager homesteads, or flocking to the towns to seek work. New labor had to be found. Other peoples were enticed to the island to work the field. These included workers from China, India, Nepal, and other countries whose descendants' diverse heritages flavor Jamaican culture today.

Although Jamaica's slaves were now free, blacks

and whites were by no means equal in wealth or rights. In protest against the abject poverty in which most Jamaican blacks were forced to live, the Morant Bay Rebellion exploded in 1865, led by Paul Bogle, a Baptist preacher. The government responded to the protests like a destroying hammer: more than 400 were shot or hanged, including Bogle, and the militia leveled thousands of homes. As a result of the rebellion, Britain abolished Jamaica's 200-year-old independent assembly, and made the island a Crown Colony, ending its autonomy in domestic affairs. Jamaica would now be ruled directly by the Colonial Office in far-off London. Black Jamaicans continued to have no voice in their government; they were left to chafe under continuing white rule.

Throughout the nineteenth century and into the twentieth, Jamaica slumbered under the tropical sun. No longer the bustling hub of wealth it had been as a sugar capital or as the center of the now abolished slave trade, its economy remained primarily agricultural. The island lagged far behind in the industrial development that was bringing wealth to other nations. "Bananas joined sugar, molasses, rum, allspice, and coffee as major export crops. Plantains, nutmeg, cloves, yams, and cinnamon supplied secondary crops."[6]

During the 1930s, Jamaica was hit harder by the worldwide Depression than many other countries.

Growing unemployment, together with a disease that decimated the banana crop, heightened the discontent of the island's disenfranchised black population. In 1938, that discontent erupted into rioting and violence that ultimately resulted in the establishment of political parties for the first time in Jamaica's history. Alexander Bustamente formed the Labour Party and Norman Manley founded the People's National Party. Under the leadership of Bustamente and Manley, the Jamaican constitution was rewritten in 1944. The new constitution granted universal suffrage at last, and put an end to the Crown Colony system of government in Jamaica. It was not until nearly twenty years later, however, that Jamaica finally achieved full independence from Great Britain in 1962.

Although, by the 1960s, Jamaica was free of British rule, had established political parties, and had extended the vote to its black citizens, most of these continued to languish in poverty, scraping a subsistence from the small farms they owned or crowding into the ghettos of Kingston and other cities. Politics frequently provided an arena for the relief of frustration through violence, and followers of the competing parties campaigned as often by violence as by rhetoric. Power was still in the hands of the white minority, while the majority continued to seek economic and political justice.

Yet the island's distinctive spirit survived. As one reggae artist, Edward Brathwaite, said, "Jamaica: fragment of bomb-blast, catastrophe of geological history (volcano, middle passage, slavery, plantation, colony, neo-colony) has somehow miraculously—some say triumphantly—survived. How we did this is still a mystery and perhaps it should remain so. But at least we can say this: that the secret and expression of the survival lies glittering and vibrating in our music."[7] That music has many roots in the past of Jamaica, particularly in the spiritual beliefs that buoyed up the hopes of those Jamaicans who suffered and endured.

2 MARCUS GARVEY AND RASTAFARIANISM

I dream, mon, every Rastamon's dream, to fly home
to Ethiopia and leave a-Babylon, where de politicians
doan let I an' I brethren be free an' live we own
righteous way.
                                                    —Bob Marley[1]

RELIGION IN JAMAICA HAS ALWAYS BEEN A POTPOURRI
of beliefs drawn from several cultures. The slaves
from Africa were forced to adopt Christianity by
their owners, both Spanish and British. However,
they fused Christianity with their own beliefs, and
some of the practices that resulted survive to this
day. "Cults still practiced by a few—or which have
contributed elements to Afro-Christian sects—
include *Obeah* and *Myal* (sorcery), and [the] related
cults *Kumina* (meaning to move with rhythm) and
Bongo, which believe in the power of *duppies*
(ghosts), and use drumming, dancing and spiritual

19

trances. . . . African beliefs merged with the Baptist faith [in the nineteenth century] to produce the Revival movement, with sects like *Pocomania*."[2] The most recent movement to emerge from this diverse mixture of cultures and beliefs is that of Rastafarianism.

When most non-Jamaicans think of a Rastafarian, they picture someone with long, ropelike dreadlocks smoking ganja (marijuana) and playing reggae music. But these are merely the superficial characteristics of the religion and are also those most often adopted by "false Rastas," those "who adopt the style without the real commitment . . . 'Him [who]

have locks on head but not in heart.'"[3] Rastafarianism is much more than dreadlocks and reggae. It is a religion, a way of life, and a movement of social protest dating back to the 1920s, when Rastafarianism was born out of the poverty and heartbreak of the Jamaican ghettos to inspire black people everywhere.

Marcus Mosiah Garvey was born in St. Ann's Bay,

Marcus Garvey

Jamaica, on August 17, 1887. Growing up poor in Jamaica taught Garvey that black people needed political and economic power to overcome the injustice they suffered. In 1916, Garvey traveled to New York City to recruit followers in a new cause, the Universal Negro Improvement Association, formed to awaken black consciousness and pride and to advocate for a "back to Africa" movement. The movement's goal was to establish a new country in Africa to which peoples from all parts of the African diaspora could go and live in unity. As Garvey said, "Our desire is for a place in the world, not to distort the tranquility of other men, but to lay down our burden and rest our weary backs and feet by the banks of the Niger and sing our songs and chant our hymns to the God of Ethiopia."[4] This desire was embodied in his black nationalist slogan: "One Aim, One God, One Destiny."

Although Garvey's back-to-Africa idea had little appeal for many of his listeners or to the readers of his newspaper, *Negro World*, his themes of economic independence and black pride were enthusiastically received by African Americans who were suffering from the restraints and cruelties of the Jim Crow laws then prevalent in the United States. In the period of reaction that followed Reconstruction, blacks, although free, were still oppressed by restrictive laws that denied them equality with the white population.

In the South, transportation, public facilities, and even jobs were segregated by race. Poll taxes kept many blacks from even exercising their right to vote. Segregation, especially in the schools, was widespread in the North also. Garvey advocated full freedom and equality of opportunity, and enticed many to his cause. By the 1920s, the Universal Negro Improvement Association had 5 million members in various countries.[5] Garvey did eventually convince a number of his followers to support his back-to-Africa idea. His attempt to implement this idea, though, led to his downfall in the United States.

Calling himself "Provisional President of Africa, Commander of the Order of the Nile, Distinguished Son of Ethiopia," Garvey organized a steamship company, the Black Star Line, that was to transport blacks from around the world to a new independent state in Africa. However, "of the three ships operated two went aground and the third was seized to meet claims of $100,000. Garvey continued to solicit passage money to Africa after he had no ships."[6] Garvey sold shares in the company to supporters of his back-to-Africa scheme, hoping to rebuild his steamship line, but in 1923, he and three associates were charged and convicted of using the U.S. mails for fraudulent purposes, and were sentenced to five years in prison. In 1927, his sentence was commuted by President Calvin Coolidge, and he was deported to Jamaica, his dreams of establishing a new African nation in ruins but his dreams of equality intact. As he left the United States, he said, "I leave America fully as happy as when I came. . . . The program of Nationalism is as important as it ever was. . . . The program I represent is not hostile to the white race or any other race. All that I want to do is to complete the freedom of the Negro economically and culturally and make him a full man. . . ."[7]

Although Garvey did not succeed in his back-to-Africa movement, he was successful in his own country of Jamaica as a voice of black empowerment—and as a prophet. In 1927, shortly after his return from the United States, Garvey gave a speech in a Kingston church. In it, he said, "Look to Africa, where a black king shall be crowned."[8]

Emperor Haile Selassie on the throne at his coronation

Ras Tafari Makonnen (1892–1975) was crowned Emperor of Ethiopia on November 2, 1930. His full title was His Imperial Majesty Emperor Haile Selassie I, King of Kings, Lord of Lords, Conquering Lion of Judah, Elect of God, Light of the World. The name Haile Selassie means "Power of the Trinity," and those who had heard a prophecy in Garvey's words announced that the Redeemer, the Black Messiah, or even "Jah" (God) had come, and that Ethiopia was the promised land to which the lost black tribes of Israel would someday return. They found justification for the belief of Haile Selassie's divinity in the Bible (Revelation 5:5): "'Do not weep; for the Lion from the tribe of Judah, the

Portrait of Ethiopian emperor Haile Selassie with the royal family

Scion of David, has won the right to open the scroll and break its seven seals.'" The Rastafari movement had begun.

Rastafarianism was bolstered in 1937 when Haile Selassie's cousin, Dr. Malaku Bayen, organized the Ethiopian World Federation (EWF) in New York City to support Ethiopia, which was being invaded by Italy at that time. By the following year, a Jamaican branch of the EWF had been founded and many Rastafarians in Jamaica were finding inspiration in its newspaper, *The Voice of Ethiopia*.

Garvey himself did not admire Haile Selassie, condemned the slavery that still existed in Ethiopia at the time, and thought the Rastafarians were fanatics.[9] With his Universal Negro Improvement Association in disarray in the United States, Garvey moved to England in 1935, where he continued to promote his international movement until his death in 1940. Those who had found religious inspiration in his earlier words ignored Garvey's opinions about Rastafarianism and viewed him as a prophet, pointing out that even John the Baptist had doubts about Jesus.

Although, from 1930 through the 1960s, Rastafarianism was primarily confined to Jamaica, and was dominated by a number of "elders," each of whom seemed to promote his own beliefs, often in conflict with those of others, the religion was seen by its adherents as a means of salvation:

> In the depressed 1930s, the poor folk of Jamaica were ready for a new religion of hope. Its adherents live according to a code which includes living in harmony with *Jah* (God), believing everyone is equal, opposing greed and exploitation, desiring no more than the essentials of life, not eating meat and shellfish (or drinking alcohol), [and] Bible reading. . . . [10]

Rastafarians (Rastas) have little formal organization and may vary in the customs they follow. All, however, hold two basic beliefs: "(1) that Haile Selassie I . . . is the living God, and (2) that Africa is the real home of the black man; his paradise. They see themselves as the lost children of Israel captive in Babylon, awaiting deliverance. . . ."[11] The term "Babylon" is used variously to refer to white society, to the United States or Western influence, to the police, or to all that is corrupting in the world. Although peaceful in nature, Rastafarianism is, in essence, a resistance and freedom movement with a religious core. Rastafarians claim that white preachers and missionaries perverted the Bible to hide the fact that Adam and Jesus were black in order to keep blacks in subjugation.

The most distinctive feature of many Rastafarians is their dreadlock hairstyle. This custom, they believe, is decreed by the Bible (Numbers 6:5): "During the whole term of his vow no razor shall touch his head; he shall let his hair grow long and plait it until he has completed the term of his dedication: he shall keep himself holy to the Lord." The hairstyle, thought by many to symbolize a lion's mane, is also inspired both by one of Haile Selassie's titles, "Lion of Judah," and by some traditional African hairstyles. Not all Rastafarians wear dreadlocks, however, and the styles of those who do wear them vary greatly:

> Many are "locksmen," wearing their hair in plaits, which they themselves smear with lard [sic], called "dreadlocks," often for convenience stuffing the mass of hair into large woolen caps, frequently in the red, green, and gold [sic] of Ethiopia. Other Rastas are "beardsmen," keeping the hair short above but allowing "no razor upon the beard." Some Rastas have both locks and beards, and some are "baldheads."[12]

One of the most controversial features of Rastafarianism is the smoking of ganja (marijuana) by many of its followers. Marijuana was first brought to the island by workers who were imported from India in the mid-1800s; *ganja* is the Hindi word for the plant. "For generations in Jamaica, ganja has been not only smoked, but brewed as tea and eaten as seasoning in soups and stews . . . [but] for Rastas, ganja—'herb'—has sacramental importance."[13] Rastafarians believe that smoking ganja brings them closer to Jah, aids in meditation, and opens their consciousness to themselves and to the world. Ganja is usually smoked in a cigarette form, called a 'spliff,' or from a pipe that has been blessed, called a 'chalice.' When smoked in a chalice or chillum pipe as a form or worship, it is solemnly passed in strict religious observance from one person to the other as a holy sacrament. . . . This ritual, referred to as 'licking the chalice' or 'sipping from the cup,' is comparable to the Christian communion rite."[14] Although many associate Rastafarianism with smoking ganja, just as not all Rastas affect dreadlocks, not all Rastas smoke herb.

While all native Jamaicans speak a thick patois that mixes words from African and other languages with those of English, Rastafarians speak a unique dialect that attempts to differentiate the "godly from the ungodly."[15] One defining characteristic of this dialect that is often confusing is its idiosyncratic use of the word *I*:

There is the mystifying tendency of Rastas to use the nominative case exclusively: "I," "I and I," "I and I brethren." This extends to the substitution of an *I* prefix for the first syllable of a word, e.g.: "I-dren" (children) or "I-tal" (natural). Reggae songs are literally peppered with Rasta slogans such as "I-Ree-Ites" ("Higher Heights," or perhaps "Israelites").[16]

Jamaican patois is a Creole dialect and is known as Jamaica Talk. In the ghettos of Jamaica, "Dread Talk" emerged in the twentieth century, combining Jamaican patois with the Rasta idea of "word-sound-power," in which all words are believed to be ways of communicating both personal and religious power. Dread Talk employs *I-* and *I and I* as a sign of adherence to Rastafarianism, and to separate the speaker and his or her beliefs from the world of Babylon. In addition, the use of *I and I* indicates a union between *Jah,* "I" and oneself "I."

Initially, as in most new religions, the Rastafarian movement in Jamaica was small and somewhat obscure. From the 1930s through the 1950s, the majority of Rastafarians lived close to nature in encampments in the mountainous interior of Jamaica. The most renowned settlement was known as Pinnacle, begun near St. Catherine in 1940 by Leonard Howell, who was also called "Gangunguru" or "Gong," and was founded on the theme of "Peace and Love."

In 1932, Howell began preaching that poor blacks should pay allegiance to Emperor Haile Selassie I. The following year, Howell was imprisoned for trying to sell pictures of Haile Selassie, claiming that they were exclusive passports to Ethiopia. After serving a short prison sentence, Howell returned to preaching, and in 1940, led his followers into the hills that had earlier been the refuge of the Maroons, establishing the Pinnacle community "which would become a focus for Rastafarianism."[17] The Pinnacle did not last long, however; in 1941, the community was raided by the police, who closed it down and arrested seventy people for growing ganja. Most of those who had been involved in the Pinnacle relocated to the Back-a-Wall section of Kingston, a shantytown steeped in poverty that, together with Trench Town and other neighborhoods, makes up the city's sprawling ghettos. There the movement became associated with ghetto life. In the 1950s, faced with the poverty and lack of opportunity in the ghetto, some Rastafarians rejected the nonviolent teaching of the movement and mounted a series of violent uprisings. Although a 1960 study of Rastafarians in Jamaica proved the contrary, Rastas were long associated with violence and crime in the minds of many because of the actions of the small number who had resorted to violence in the 1950s.[18]

Rastafarianism continued to grow in Jamaica's cities: "By the mid-'60s it was established that there were at least 70,000 Rastafarians living in Jamaica."[19] Rastafarianism drew the poor and the disenfranchised to its ranks because of its message of black empowerment and equality. However, it was not until the 1970s that it became more than a loosely organized system of beliefs.

During the 1960s, a number of Rastafarian groups existed: the United Ethiopian Body, the Ethiopian Youth Cosmic Faith, and the Ethiopian Coptic League, among others. Each had its own version of Rastafarianism, but none exerted widespread influence. All were eclipsed in 1968, however, when the Twelve Tribes of Israel was founded in Trench Town by Vernon Carrington, who until then had been a vendor of the juices and herb-root drinks that are so popular on the island. Carrington preached that the human race was made up of twelve tribes, each named for one of Jacob's sons in the Bible, and each associated with a month of the year. Members of the Twelve Tribes of Israel "believe that one must assume the name of the biblical tribe corresponding to the month in which one's birthday falls. . . . The Twelve Tribes stress racial tolerance and freedom of lifestyle and appearances."[20] Like other Rastafarian groups, followers of the Twelve Tribes believe in eventual repatriation to Africa, and in the Bible. The Twelve Tribes owed its broad appeal and its success in attracting a wide audience to a number of well-known figures among its adherents; most notable among these was the reggae singer Bob Marley, who would soon take some of the musical traditions and beliefs of Rastafarianism and create a name for himself around the world.

With Jamaican independence in 1962 there came a need for the country to define itself, to create a national identity. Many black Jamaicans found this identity in Rastafarianism because of its messages of black pride and independence, ideas that were also being expressed with growing emphasis in the United States through its own civil rights movement. One expression of Rastafarian pride was the emergence of a musical form with both African and Jamaican roots whose lyrics expressed strong messages of social and political protest: reggae.

3
SOUNDS OUT OF AFRICA

The slaves under severely repressive conditions preserved what they could of African culture, including music and dance, capsulated in extracts from larger ritual forms of their homelands. These were rituals rich in the spiritual vitality and emotionalism that characterized the expression of the intensely religious Africans.[1]

WHEN THE AFRICAN ANCESTORS OF THOSE NOW living in Jamaica were stolen from their homes in Africa and forced aboard the ships that would carry them across the ocean to lives of slavery, they left all their material possessions behind. Frequently, they were stripped even of their clothing and made to lie for days on end, in naked misery, in the stinking holds of the slave ships. Many died on their journey across the Atlantic. Those who survived arrived in a new world half-starved and ill, their families and lives stolen from them. But although the slavers had stripped them of their families, their freedom, and their dignity, there were two things that could not be taken from them: their culture and their music.

The slaves from West Africa carried with them their musical traditions and their knowledge of drum-making. The new slaves re-created their burru drums, a family of "talking" drums, and the drummers flourished in Jamaica:

> The drum in African culture is recognized as an instrument of communication. For Africans, the drum talks. For Jamaicans, the "ridim" [rhythm] talks. . . . African traditional music is usually based on a five-note scale which gives a minor tonality to their melodies. Many traditional Jamaican songs are in minor-sounding keys.[2]

For the oppressed slaves, drumming was not only a traditional means of communication, and a way of recalling what they had lost, it was a heritage to be handed down to their children. Among the Maroons in their remote mountain hideaways, drumming was a means of preserving their heritage. In addition to drums, as Timothy White writes, "the Maroons preserved African ways in the plaintive signal codes of their multitonal 'abeng' cow horns, an instrument of warning similar to the Akan *abertia*."[3] During the centuries following, this heritage of drums and rhythms became an integral part of Jamaican music, particularly today in Kumina, an ecstatic dance done to communicate with one's ancestors, and in Nyahbinghi music.

Nyahbinghi (also Niyabingi, Nyabingi, or Nyabinghi) is the strictest order of Rastafarianism. The music used in its ceremonies, or "grounations" as they are called, includes the use of an *akete*, a drum battery consisting of a large bass drum that is beaten with a padded stick, and smaller *funde* and *repeater* hand drums. Sometimes horns and guitars are also added.[4] The rhythm and lyrics of the songs combine to express praise of Jah as well as social commentary. "Ironically, reggae isn't authentic Rasta music—Nyahbinghi drumming is. 'The rhythms [of reggae] are based on Nyahbinghi, and the lyrics are social commentary,'" according to Desta Tonge, a Jamaican musicians' agent.[5] Nyahbinghi music, chanting, and dancing were handed down directly from those who came as slaves to the island in the sixteenth century and after.

Many slaves, particularly those from Western and Central Africa, also carried with them the tradition of the *griot*. In many West African countries, male and female professional singers and storytellers, called griots, performed against a background of drumming and other musical instruments, commenting on tribal and political events in their songs. The griot's position in African society is an esteemed one:

The griots are rightly referred to as the archives and libraries of this part of Africa. Thus the famous proverb, "whenever a griot dies, a library dies." They were interpreters of current politics, transmitting messages and orders from the governing power to the people. As musicians with contacts with musicians outside the court, they were able to learn the opinion of common people and could convey sentiments of the populace to the ruler.[6]

This combination of commentary, singing, and drumming was passed on by the slaves in Jamaica and incorporated into other musical forms learned from the white population of the island. Many of the later forms of Jamaican music, including reggae, derive their rhythms from these drumming traditions, convey messages about societal conditions, and also often utilize the call-and-response technique of the griot.

In call and response, the performer sings a phrase and the audience or backup group responds either in song or by commenting upon the singer's performance or message. Call and response is also found in the United States. Early blues artists, gospel singers, preachers, and, later, rap artists have employed this device. In gospel music, the response is usually a hearty "amen" spoken or sung by the listeners; in rap music, the responses range from both flattering and insulting comments on the artist's performance by the audience or backup group, to additional raps by the backup musicians. Like the griots of old, many raps also comment on social conditions.

Jamaican slaves not only had their own musical traditions apart from the white population but quickly learned those of their white owners. Slaves were frequently forced to learn to play European musical instruments to provide music for the entertainment of the white slaveowners at dances and parties. The quadrille, a dance that originated in Europe, was particularly popular among the white overseers. Its popularity led to the formation of many quadrille bands made up of slaves. While the quadrille in Europe was a formal dance, with precise, rather stiff movements, in

Jamaicans gave quadrille dances, which came to the island from Europe, a new flavor.

Jamaica, the quadrille bands Africanized it, adding the captivating rhythms of their drums and loosening up the movements of the dance steps.

Other forms of music were also emerging as a result of this blending of musical traditions. One that is still prevalent today grew from the upsurge of Protestant religious feeling known as the Great Revival, which swept the United States and Great Britain in the nineteenth century. The Revival resulted in the establishment among the black population of Jamaica of several new religious sects, Revival Zionism and Pocomania among them. These gave rise to what is referred to as "Christian music," a kind of gospel music that, today, has close ties to reggae. "Both Revival Zion and Pocomania combined African and Christian religious elements, and involved handclapping, foot-stomping and the use of the bass drum, side drum, cymbals, and rattle."[7]

In Pocomania (or Poco), which is still practiced, Christianity is combined with African beliefs, West African deities often being identified with Christian saints. Ceremonies involve singing and dancing, the distinct drum rhythms of Poco echoing the burru drumming of the slaves of years past. The heavy Pocomania rhythms strongly influenced later Jamaican musical styles, including dancehall and reggae.

This combination of African and European musical influences also occurred in secular contexts. During the eighteenth century, in addition to slaves entertaining their owners and overseers with quadrille bands, the slaves also played their own brand of music at "Jonkanoo" (Junkonnu) celebrations. Fife-and-drums bands, originally formed to play for the entertainment of the white plantation owners, also played the music for a risqué dance favored by slaves. The dance, variously called "John Canoe," "John Connu," or "Jonkanoo," involved a group of masked dancers and was rooted in a "West Africa fertility ritual . . . associated with the yam harvest."[8] These festivals delighted both the black and white population of the island:

> The early Jonkanoo . . . celebrations, an amalgam of African, European, and what was evolving as Jamaican cultural activity, utilized drumming, rattles, and conch-blowing in elaborate bands of masqueraders who appeared at Christmas. The masqueraders, usually men, dressed as animals, devils, and women . . . [and] marched in a riotous parade. . . . Planters at first encouraged Jonkanoo celebrations, until they realized that slaves were communicating with their drums and conch shells.[9]

Jonkanoo bands played on a variety of musical instruments of both European and African origin.

Although the planters clamped down on the Jonkanoo celebrations, fearing that it encouraged slave rebellion, the Jonkanoo tradition survived. A new form of music was also emerging from a combination of the lively Jonkanoo music, earlier African rhythms, lively airs from South America, and the lilting melodies of the quadrille band: mento, Jamaica's own brand of calypso music.

Calypso music began in Trinidad. As with burru drumming and the music of the Jonkanoo, calypso rhythms came to the Caribbean from West Africa with the first slaves in the seventeenth century. "The artform . . . combines the skills of storytelling, singing, and instrument making . . . [and] usually involves some social commentary, typically a humorous satire on social and political events, with an infectious beat."[10] Calypso lyrics are usually witty and make humorous comments on social, political, or economic problems. Today, the rhythms of calypso, usually with two beats to the bar, are most often associated with the steel band's percussion instruments made from the tops of oil drums. The steel drum was developed by Ellie Mannette, "the first man to 'sink' and then tune, in raised sections, the surface of an oil drum top."[11]

In Jamaica, mento emerged in the nineteenth century as a mix of calypso from Trinidad and Tobago and the samba from Brazil, and its songs

This typical mento band uses a banjo, guitar, rhumba box, and sax to create its unique sound.

functioned in a way that was frequently similar to those of the African griots. "Mento is a song and dance form which was the métier of troubadours of the early days, who carried gossip and social commentary in lively songs and dances, playing on their mostly homemade drums, bamboo fifes, and fiddles."[12] Like the quadrille and Jonkanoo bands, mento musicians quickly began to use a variety of instruments of both European and African origin. Many mento bands included banjo, guitar, pennywhistles, and harmonica. In addition to drums, the bands would also frequently have a rhumba box (a large bass *mbira,* or "thumb piano," of South African origin), shakers, scrapers, and tambourine.

Because of its prevailing up-tempo beat and liveliness, mento resembles calypso superficially, but displays a wider range of tempos and song types. Calypso music is based on about fifty standardized melodies, while mento bands experimented with both melody and beat. "The songs were usually upbeat, humorous accounts of daily, and often sexual, life."[13] Calypso was an "exact science, a sophisticated vehicle for social comment," but mento was "often crude and dirty, so lewd in fact, that the church in Jamaica kept some of the best mento recordings from being sold except under the counter."[14] In spirit, though not in form or rhythm, mento is also sometimes compared to the early Delta blues.

The two music forms—calypso and mento—became confused with one another in the minds of many in the 1950s when calypso music became popular in the United States. Since calypso was the type of music they expected of Caribbean musicians, tourists thought it was calypso that Jamaican bands were playing at the large hotels on the island's north coast, and for the passengers on the cruise ships frequenting Montego Bay and Kingston harbor, but usually the music was mento. This confusion was reinforced by the popularity in the United States of singer Harry Belafonte. White tourists came to believe such Belafonte songs as "Jamaican Farewell" (which is actually a mento song) and "The Banana Boat Song" epitomized the music of Jamaica and of

all the islands. These songs, however, hardly repre-
sented Jamaican music as a whole, or even the more
modern mento music which, as Timothy White
notes, was "an aggressive amalgam that also con-
tained South African elements and a percussive tack
similar to the highlife music of Nigeria."[15]

Such mento music as was recorded was not widely
heard in the United States. Most mento records were
made and distributed primarily in Jamaica and in
England, which had a large emigrant population from
the island. In 1951, band leader and jazz musician
Bertie King recorded Harold Robinson and the
Ticklers in appliance-store owner Stanley Motta's

Harry Belafonte recording at RCA Studios in 1957

recording studio. They produced a 78 record with "Don't Fence Her In" on one side, and "Glamour Girl" on the other. The record, which was manufactured by Emil Shallit (who later began the Kalypso label) and distributed by Decca Records in Great Britain, proved popular with both islanders and those who had moved to England. To the latter, the music was a taste of home away from home. The disc's success led others to produce more mento records. Stanley Motta began producing and distributing mento records on his MRS (Motta's Recording Studio) label. Caribou records, founded by Baba Tuari, followed, as did Jamaican R & B, and Federal records, founded by Ken Khouri.

Mento was lively, appealing, and humorous; it was fun to listen to, great to dance to. Mento songs, for the most part, did not reflect the desperate living conditions of the majority of Jamaicans, or the social protest movement that was simmering beneath the surface of the sunlit island. One of the few exceptions to this rule was musician Lord Lebby's song, "Ethiopia," "one of the first expressions of Rastafarian consciousness on record."[16] "Ethiopia" used the rhythms of mento to express the ever-present desire of the Rastafarians to return to the "homeland" of Ethiopia.

Jamaican music had some distance to travel, however, before this sentiment would emerge forcefully in the music known as reggae. Mento remained essentially a rural art form, Jamaica's folk music. In the 1940s and '50s, while tourists swayed to calypso and mento beats, mainstream Jamaican music was evolving in another direction in the hands of those running their own huge "sound systems."

4
BIG SOUNDS, BIG SYSTEMS

Singles [records] . . . came at you first in a sound system dance or in the cramped confines of Musick City in Ridley Road, Dalston, or Paul's in Finsbury Park, or Desmon's Hip City in Brixton. In each case you would have felt them as much as heard them. The bass boomed out of speakers so big you could raise a family in them and thumped you firmly in the guts.[1]

DURING THE PERIOD BETWEEN THE TWO WORLD wars, Jamaicans became enthralled by the music heard over various radio stations broadcasting from the United States, the records brought in both by sailors stopping at the island, and by those returning Jamaicans who had traveled to the United States or England seeking work. Big-band sounds may have filled the air in the wealthier quarters of the island, but American rhythm and blues was the music that captured the hearts of everyday Jamaicans. After World War II, R & B took over completely. With its heavy beat, it was music that could be danced to, sung to, and everyone wanted to hear it, but local Jamaican radio stations, which were government controlled, played conservative music, not what the people really wanted to hear. As a result, "sound systems" began to spring up around the island:

> The very early sound systems were fairly basic, comprising one record deck, a valve amp, and the largest commercially available loudspeakers. As the 1950s progressed, however, they became more powerful and technically sophisticated, to the extent that a sound system's theme tune was audible several streets away.[2]

The early sounds systems were meant to share the music that was *hot*, and as loudly as possible. Today's sound systems are much more elaborate, and inevitably, more technically advanced:

> The equipment for a sound system is called a set. This includes turntables, mixers, tape decks, CD mixers, echo chambers, amplifiers, speakers, power supplies, wires and cords, storage and travel parcels, and backup equipment. Each system may own thousands of records and CDs, and a good one may own out-of-print valuable records. . . .[3]

The sound systems played, and still play, in various bars and dance halls and in open areas called "lawns." Because they were often set up outdoors and were designed to attract as many listeners and dancers as possible, the sound system business became extremely competitive. The larger and louder a system, the newer the records, and the better the DJ, the better chance it had of drawing people from other systems set up nearby, so rivalries and "battles" between sound systems developed.

For the bar and dance-hall owners, sound systems proved to be a boon. Not only could good systems capture patrons, they were cheaper than live bands. As one dance-hall owner, Bunny Lee, said,

"Y'see, after the orchestra play all an hour, dem stop fi a break an' dem eat off all the curry goat, an' drink off all the liquor. So the promoter never mek no profit—dem did prove too expensive fi the dance promoter. Dem alone eat a pot of goat! So when sound came now, the sound no tek no break. When these few sound system come, it was something different...."[4]

Unlike an orchestra or band, sound systems usually had only a DJ or MC to play the records and comment on them, a selector to pick out records, and a number of other people to help transport, set up, and protect the system; as the systems became more competitive, many hired "enforcers" to make sure people paid to listen to the music, and to stop fights. Even so, the sound system crews numbered far fewer members than the big bands that had grown in popularity during the war years. And their music was more current and easier to dance to.

Certain sound systems, understandably, began to be more widely known and became more popular than others. The most popular not only had the latest, largest—and loudest—equipment, but the latest records. Owners of sound systems would try anything to get the best records to play, and to keep them away from their competitors. If a system owner managed to get hold of a record popular with the crowds, he might scratch off the label, rename the song, or paste on a false label to keep his competitors from discovering the song's title and its producer. Sound-system owners went to great length to get the best records, traveling to the United States and ferreting out both popular records and obscure recordings put out by small labels that were unlikely to have been heard on the radio.

In the battle of the sound systems during the 1950s, several systems emerged triumphant over their competitors. One of these belonged to Duke Reid, who, together with his fierce competitors, Clement "Sir Coxsone" Dodd and "King" Edwards, later heavily influenced the development of reggae music. A fourth belonged to Cecil "Prince Buster" Bustamente Campbell.

Duke Reid was born in Jamaica in 1915, and had served as a policeman in Kingston for ten years when, in the 1950s, he and his wife Lucille bought the Treasure Isle Liquor Store. To advertise his store, Reid began hosting a radio show, *Treasure Isle Time*, playing R & B records from the United States. At this time, sound systems were starting to become a favorite form of entertainment with the young people on the island. Recognizing the popularity of both the music and of sound systems, Reid began his own system, the Trojan. The Trojan, which eventually included several systems, soon became one of the popular favorites, and was often challenged to battles by other systems. In the battles of the sound systems, Reid, who was known for carrying two guns, frequently made that battle literal. Although he tended to attract a rougher following than other systems and had a tough-guy image, Reid also had a good ear for music. Like other system owners, he traveled to the United States several times a year to search for new records for his system to play, and The Trojan became known for its originality as well as its rough edges.

In the battle of the systems, Clement "Sir Coxsone" Dodd was to emerge as the preeminent rival to Duke Reid. Born in 1932, Dodd was among the first in Jamaica to own and run his own sound system, Sir Coxsone the Downbeat. Dodd started out playing records at his parents' liquor store, Dodd's, in Kingston, and eventually set up his own system in the mid-1950s. By 1957, Dodd owned three "sets"—three sound systems—all named Sir Coxsone the Downbeat, and was a strong challenger to Duke Reid in popularity. Competition was strong, as Lee "Scratch" Perry, who worked for Dodd, remembers:

> Start time we was definitely the smallest of the systems. Duke had some big bad guys operating for him. So my job was to fight down this. . . go out and find the best sound. We go out and find them and really upset Duke and them others. It come up we start to have top record all the while and sometime we meet other systems in a club, slug it out toe for toe. Soon we a top shape.[5]

The systems of Dodd and Reid each had their own, deeply devoting following of fans. Fans of each system developed such strong allegiance to their system that they would not listen to the system of the other. Sometimes, two systems would play the same dance hall, set up on stages opposite

Lee Perry

each other, and "battle" with each other. Then, each would play its loudest, trying to draw fans and dancers away from its rival with ear-blasting insistence.

Vincent "King" Edwards started the King Edwards the Giant sound system in 1955, rising quickly in popularity to challenge Dodd and Reid for the position of top system in Kingston. "I started off with a fifty-watt amplifier, made with seven or eight tubes," Edwards says. "The first night I played at Galloway Road, I played against a sound called Cavalier, and I was flopped. So I had to regroup myself, build a bigger sound."[6] With a bigger system, Edwards was quickly able to "flop" his competitors (outplay their system) and take the lead among the systems in his area of Kingston, eventually owning seven sets.

A fourth figure on the sound-system scene who rose above the crowd was Cecil Bustamante Campbell, known as Prince Buster, who was born in Kingston in 1938. Named after the founder and leader of the Jamaican Labour Party, Alexander Bustamante, Campbell was a boxer who was hired by Coxsone Dodd as a bouncer and protector of Dodd's sound system. "Competition was fierce in the early days, with fights frequently breaking out between the supporters of rival sounds, and with wires (and people) being cut regularly."[7] Campbell provided the muscle to protect Dodd's system against this violence. Caught up in both the scene and music, in 1957 Campbell opened the Prince Buster Record Shack on Charles Street in Kingston, and around 1959, as Prince Buster, he set up his own sound system, Voice of the People.

As the sound systems became a way of nightlife in Jamaica, those running and working for them began to attain a notoriety of their own. The DJs at first began sprinkling an enticing patter of "jive" in the manner of radio disk jockeys as they changed records, and then started developing their own lines and "raps." One of the first "talkers," Count Machuki recalls,

I came into Clement Dodd, who was Sir Coxsone. . . . I said to Mr. Dodd: "Give me the microphone." And he handed me the mike, I started dropping my wisecracks, and Mr. Dodd was all for it. And I started trying my phrases on Coxsone, and he gave me one or two wisecracks, too. . . . Then I was passing Beverley's record shop, and I see a magazine called *Jive*. . . . And from there on, I was able to create my own jives. The first I wrote for myself was: "If you dig my jive/You're cool and very much alive/Everybody all round town/Machuki's the reason why I shake it down/When it comes to jive/You can't whip him with no stick."[8]

The "wisecracks" and "jive" that began with DJs such as Machuki would later be transported to the United States to influence the evolution of America's

rap music of the 1970s and after. On the island, indi-
vidual DJs, often also called MCs (masters of ceremonies), became recognized for their artistry with
their sound systems and for their skills in "toasting"
and "boasting," talking over records and selections
of records, eventually creating what became known
as "dancehall" in the 1980s.

Jamaican-born Clive Campbell, known as "Kool
Herc" (short for Hercules), is credited with bringing
similar techniques to New York when he and his
family moved to the United States in the early 1970s.
Around 1973, Campbell began to put together a
sound system in the Bronx like those in Jamaica, and
in 1975, he started to play at various clubs and
dances. During his performances as Kool Herc,
Campbell would throw in rhymes and comments as
did the Jamaican sound-system DJs. Like them, too,
he exhibited a real flair for experimentation with his
sound system:

> Kool Herc seldom played an entire song. He knew which part of
> the record sent his audience into a frenzy. It was usually a 30-
> second "break" section in which the drums, bass, and rhythm
> guitar stripped the beat to its barest essence. Herc used two
> turntables to accomplish this feat. This technique became
> known as "beats" or "break-beats."[9]

With these "breaks," a style of dancing emerged to take advantage of the strong beat, one that showcased the dancer's acrobatic skills: break dancing. As DJs or MCs began to creatively combine different beats and expand on their talking while playing the records, rap music emerged in the United States as a defined style of music.

In the Jamaica of the 1950s, years before Kool Herc's innovations, sound systems continued to evolve. Competition was fierce between the systems. Those with the latest R & B and doo-wop records from the States were the most popular. Top system owners such as Clement Dodd, Prince Buster, King Edwards, and Duke Reid continued to spend thousands of dollars traveling to the United States several times a year to get the latest in American music to play to keep their systems on top. But as the decade progressed, American music was moving on, and the heavy beat of R & B evolved into the smoother tones of soul music. Jamaican audiences, though, demanded that beat; the weighty pulse amplified through the huge speakers of a sound system drew dancers like flies and assured that the system with the best beat would dominate the others. As soul music slowed the beat down, Jamaicans began rocking to the sounds of New Orleans artists who had an infectious beat of their own:

> It was a strutting, half-stepping "second line" approach to R & B, the tempo incorporating the New Orleans-based dirges and jump-for-joy perambulations of jazz funerals; the Latin-tinged bass patterns of cat-house pianists like Jelly Roll Morton; rhumba, samba and the mambo of Perex Prado; the barrelhouse boogie-woogie of Kid Stormy Weather . . . and the chant-along exultations of the traditional Mardi Gras fraternal societies.[10]

The problem was that although Jamaican dancers loved the New Orleans beat in records by such artists as Fats Domino or Huey Smith and the Clowns, there were only so many records available, and each system wanted to have the newest, the best, to out-draw the other systems. To assure a steady stream of such music, the owners of the top sound systems began making their own records, recording "dub plates" for use with their own systems:

> A dub plate is simply an acetate cut onto a plastic-coated metal disc, featuring an unusual mix of a well-known record, or a recording unavailable elsewhere, and used by a sound system to help to promote the exclusivity of the music it plays.[11]

The dub plate was a record made for the exclusive use of a particular sound system. As certain songs became popular, however, audiences wanted their own copies, and suddenly, sound-system owners found themselves in the record business.

In 1954, Ken Khouri started Jamaica's first record company, "Federal Records," which produced licensed copies of American recording artists and a few local artists. Clement Dodd thought this was the way to go, and began playing dub plates made by local musicians on his Worldisc label. As audiences began to demand copies of the records played by his system, Dodd edged into the record business, rather by accident. He said, "I didn't realize that this could be a business. I just did it for enjoyment."[12] As the Jamaican recording industry grew, Dodd's labels became more prominent; his Studio One label, in particular, became known not only on the island, but also in Great Britain.

Duke Reid, not one to let anyone get ahead of him, also began recording for his sound system and eventually had three labels: Treasure Island (the most famous), Dutchess, and Trojan. Reid had a real ear for music and for what the audience liked, and his records were among some of the most popular of the 1960s both in Jamaica and in England.

Prince Buster promoted his Voice of the People records through his sound system and record shop. One of his first records, "Oh Carolina," sung by the Folkes Brothers, and accompanied by Count Ossie, has become a Jamaican musical classic. Eventually,

Prince Buster had two other labels in addition to his
Voice of the People: Wild Bells, and Buster's Record
Shack. Unlike Reid and Dodd, Buster, in addition to
recording some of the top musicians in Jamaica, also
recorded himself on his labels. His songs, "Al
Capone" and "Madness" became popular at home
and in England, and in the mid-1960s, when he
toured Great Britain, he was welcomed enthusiastically by crowds of young people who were caught
up in his music: "He recorded in many different
styles, but his talking records were the most popular,
including the hilarious 'Judd Dread,' in which he
admonishes rude boys."[13]

Although King Edwards dominated the sound-
system scene around 1955, when system owners
began producing records, he later began to lag. In the
late 1950s, he began producing records on his King
Edwards label, but in the mid-1960s, he shifted his
focus to politics. He was elected a member of the
Jamaican parliament for the People's National Party
and began breeding champion racehorses, and with-
drew from the music scene.

With a burgeoning record industry, Jamaican
artists finally had an outlet for their music, and an
enthusiastic audience both on the island and among
emigrant populations in the United States, and especially in Great Britain. Talent shows were held
throughout the island, and regular audition times

were established by record-label owners to find new musicians and singers. One label which was to dominate the island and the British record scene was Island Records, which not only recorded its own artists, but also eventually distributed the labels of other companies in England and around the world.

Island Records was founded by Chris Blackwell, a distant relative of the Blackwells who managed the wealthy Crosse and Blackwell food empire of Great Britain. Blackwell was born in England. His family moved to Jamaica when he was six months old, settling in wealthy Terra Nova. When he was three years old, Blackwell was sent back to England to attend school at Harrow, but, being a poor student, he failed to gain admission to any university. In the late 1950s, an incident occurred that changed his life:

> During the summer of 1958 he was stranded on a coral reef near the Hellshire Beaches [of Jamaica]. Dehydrated and sunburnt, he was rescued by members of a small Rastafarian community, and this formative incident influenced in later life his willingness to deal directly with Rasta musicians and to introduce their philosophy and culture to European and American audiences.[14]

After dabbling in film, in 1962 Blackwell founded Island Records in London, and began leasing records from various island recording companies for distribution in England. Gradually, Island Records established a number of subsidiary labels, including Jump Up, Black Swan, and Sue, among others, which also recorded and distributed records. Although Island Records recorded a large number of Jamaican artists, including reggae artists Jimmy Cliff and Bob Marley, and later, such popular musicians as Cat Stevens, its first big success came in 1964 with Millie Small's record, "My Boy Lollipop," the first international hit by a Jamaican artist. "My Boy Lollipop" sold 6 million records and made Blackwell's recording business a viable competitor with the older, more established recording companies in both Great Britain and the United States.

Jamaica was jumping. By the 1950s and '60s, its music had generated recording studios, an abundance of musicians and singers, and outlets in the United States and Great Britain. And that music was evolving, developing into something that was uniquely Jamaican. In the early years of the recording studios, artists had at first emulated

Millie Small

the R & B and doo-wop of the United States, but they rapidly began to imprint their own signatures on it:

> The more adventurous took the nuts and bolts of the sound and melded them with energetic jazz conceits—particularly in the ever-present horn section—and emerged around 1956 with a hybrid concoction christened 'ska.'[15]

As the music changed, the new, uniquely Jamaican sounds of, first, ska, and then, rock steady, emerged.

5
JAMAICAN BEATS: SKA AND ROCK STEADY

Not *boom, boom, boom*. It is more like *chi-boom, chi-boom*. Come down easy on the offbeat, like a rhythmic shrug of the shoulders. Kind of bluesy. Kind of calypso. Kind of fun.[1]

WHILE BLACK AMERICAN MUSIC OF THE 1960s WAS smoothing into the sounds of soul, Jamaican audiences were demanding more rhythm, and a "jump" beat that could be danced to more wildly than that heard in earlier R & B and rock and roll. Since sound-system owners had, for the most part, abandoned the custom of getting new music from the United States and were recording records on a variety of their own labels, it was easy for them to give their audiences what they wanted. The result was "a hybrid of doo-wop, R & B, and jazz that eventually precipitated ska, the jump-up sound where the

62

jump took precedence over everything else."[2] Ska
(the name derives from a certain kind of electric-
guitar sound)—a combination of swing, R & B,
jazz, and mento that transcended its sources—
would dominate the Jamaican musical scene from
1961 until 1967. It was Jamaica's own homegrown
music:

> Ska. Even the name is a sound—the sound of a strategically placed
> rhythm guitar upchop transforming a rhythm and blues-based
> Latin jazz shuffle into a new musical order. Before ska, Jamaican
> music is mainly derived—the burro drumming from Africa, the
> quadrille from England, and mento, second cousin to Trinidad's
> calypso, all contain Jamaican elements grafted onto other music.[3]

Ska came just as Jamaica's recording industry was
hitting its stride. Prince Buster decided that his
records and sound systems needed something new
and different. First, he asked his guitarist, Jah Jerry,
to change the stress of the rhythm from the downbeat to the offbeat (resulting in a fast version of the
rhythm that is now associated with reggae). Like
rock and roll's backbeat, ska rhythm stressed the second and fourth beats of each bar. With the addition
of sophisticated jazz riffs, ska was born. The grandfather of reggae, ska captivated audiences and kept
them dancing with its hypnotic rhythms:

Ska—a bright propulsive style with a sensual bounce—draws from rhythm and blues, jazz and Jamaican folk music and is paced by a choppy guitar and punchy brass accents. . . . "The term *ska* was invented . . . by [bassist] Cluet Johnson, the leader of the Blues Blasters. [according to Tommy McCook, a member of the Skatalites] His nickname was Skavoovee . . . and since he was instrumental in creating the music, that's the way it had to be."[4]

One of the first groups to gain prominence in ska was the aptly named Skatalites. Prince Buster had found success with his new sound and it was quickly adopted by Sir Coxsone Dodd. Dodd initially issued ska records by the Maytals (made up of Frederick "Toots" Hibbert, Nathaniel "Jerry" Mathias/McCarthy, and Henry "Raleigh" Gordon), and by singer Delroy Wilson, whose ska lyrics often combined the religious themes found in gospel with a ska beat. With Dodd, the Maytals recorded such hits as "He Will Provide" and "Shining Light." The Maytals left Dodd,

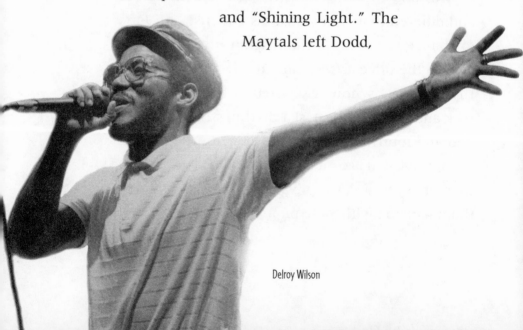

Delroy Wilson

though, because he did not pay them enough, and began recording for other labels, including Prince Buster's Wild Bells and Islam labels. In 1964, the Maytals' "Light of the World," "Judgment Day," and "He Is Real" became hits, and other groups imitated them.

In response to the success of the Maytals after their defection from his label, Dodd put together a group of musicians who were considered some of the best in the business. The Skatalites, whose members would come and go over the period of its recording lifetime, included tenor saxophonist Roland Alphonso, trombonist Rico Rodriguez, pianist Aubrey Adams, Lloyd Knibbs on drums, Jerome "Jah Jerry" Hines on calypso guitar, and bandleader and tenor saxophonist Tommy McCook, among others. According to McCook, "We were all session musicians, and people liked what we did and were always asking who did what on the records, so I proposed to form a band. . . . The name of the band is a blend of *ska* and *satellites*, a passion of the day."[5] The Skatalites would not only create some of the most popular ska music, but would also later back up Jimmy Cliff, Desmond Dekker, and reggae great Bob Marley.

Ska spread beyond Jamaica through the British recording studio of Chris Blackwell. He bought up ska tapes in Jamaica and released them in Britain.

By fortune or fluke, Blackwell "scored a huge U.S. hit in 1964 with [Millie Small's] 'My Boy Lollipop,' which showcased the guitar of Skatalite Ernest Ranglin. . . ."[6] Ska had earned its place in musical history, and generated its own form of dance, "skanking." Although that it was soon to be over-shadowed by other musical forms in Jamaica and elsewhere, even today ska continues to have a devoted following.

At the same time ska was conquering Jamaica and gaining popularity in Great Britain, where it was called "bluebeat" after the British record label Blue-Beat, Kingston and all of Jamaica were confronting the problems generated by the poverty indigenous to Trench Town and other slums. After World War II, people had flocked from the country to the cities seeking work, money, and a better life. But most found in the slums of Kingston and other cities a kind of hardship unknown in the country-side. In the country, people could at least grow their own food and barter it. The city did not offer that, and jobs were few and far between. The hope that had accompanied the freedom from British rule in the 1960s had also disappeared as it became clear that independence was not going to solve Jamaica's many problems, particularly those of the thousands who lived in poverty in its cities. Overcrowded, steeped in frustration and poverty, the slums bred groups called "rude boys" or "rud-ies," who formed political gangs, and whose heroes were legendary criminals like Vincent "Ivanhoe" Martin,

the twenty-four-year-old Kingston gunman who came to be known as "Rhyging," patois for "angry," "wild," "foolhardy." Arriving in the city from St. Catherine at fourteen as a stowaway in the back of a produce van, he was a five-foot-three black dandy who wore elevator shoes, two side pistols, and a permanent scowl. He became a ghetto folk hero after escaping from the General Penitentiary in April 1948. Several sensational shooting matches in West Kingston ensued, and Rhyging . . . vowed he would never be taken alive. A massive manhunt led to the raffish murderer's demise in a hail of police bullets on Lime Cay Beach.[7]

Martin was to became the model for many of the rudies; later, Jimmy Cliff's 1973 film *The Harder They Come*, which introduced reggae to America, used ele-ments of Martin's legend.

While ska continued to be popular, it did not speak the language of the ghetto. As the need for expression grew, musicians began to feel the rude boys' influence, and by 1966 a new musical style known as rock steady emerged. Rock steady was almost the opposite of ska:

rock steady was ... more refined and, most of all, cooler ... in rock steady the bass didn't play on every beat with equal emphasis, but rather played a repeated pattern that syncopated the rhythm. In turn, the bass and drums became much more prominent, with the horns taking on a supportive rather than lead role.[8]

In rock steady, the light, upbeat lyrics of ska turned dark, reflecting the problems, fears, and attitudes of the rudies, and glamorizing the heroes of the ghettos. The beat was slower, to match the rudies'

way of dancing slowly and menacingly. Rock-steady hits of the times included "Rudie in Court," "Rudie Get Offa Circuit Charge," "See Dem a Come," and "Rudie O Rudie." But rock steady, which was rooted in American Soul music and doo-wop, also provided the opportunity to express more tender emotions, resulting in a number of sensuous love songs by a variety of Jamaican groups. It was the music of the young. Bob Marley, whose rudie or street name was Tuff Gong, later said,

Bob Marley performing in London, 1980

Da guys who were in control robbed da older musicians up. . . .
Dem get frustrated an' stop playin'. So de music changed from da
older musicians ta de younger, hungrier ones. People like I, we
love James Brown an' love your funky stuffs, an' we dig inta dat
American bag. We didn't wan' ta stand around playin' dat slower
ska beat anymore. De young musicians, deh had a different beat—
dis was rock steady now! Eager ta go! . . . Rock steady goin'
t'rough![9]

The young groups that had been dabbling with
ska took to rocky steady eagerly. Bob Marley himself
easily adapted to rock steady, recording such songs
as "Put It On," "Rude Boy," "Good Good Rudie," and
"Let Him Go (Rude Boy Get Bail)."

At the same time that ska rode the airwaves from
1960 to 1967, with rock steady gradually overtaking
it, another musical trend was emerging in the background. In 1959, Prince Buster had taken a chance
on recording some of the singers and musicians who
were Rastas. He first approached the Rasta percus-
sionist Count Ossie (Williams) to see if he would
provide backup for some of his groups. The result
was the Folkes Brothers (John, Mico, and Junior
Folkes) whose hit "Oh Carolina" was backed by the
Nyahbinghi drumming of Count Ossie and his five
drummers, "described variously as the Warrickas,
his African Drums, or his Afro-Combo."[10] "Though

the song is fundamentally a standard R & B, driven by a pumping piano sound and doo-wop styled vocals, it is set apart by the burru drumming by Count Ossie."[11] Following the success of this record, Prince Buster began regularly recording Rasta musicians.

Initially, radio stations refused to play the records that featured Rasta musicians, claiming that they were "blasphemous," but people were buying them in the record stores, and finally the stations had to take notice or lose their listeners. Even Buster's rival, Coxsone Dodd, took note. Dodd, however, initially limited the Rasta records he issued at that time (1961–1962) to instrumentals, saying, "Sweet vocal groups de t'ing. . . . De Sound System wan' a sweet beat."[12] The Rasta rhythms, however, quickly were adopted first by ska artists, then rock-steady groups, and Dodd began using Rasta musicians to back up the various groups recording under his labels, which now numbered five—World Disc, Coxsone, Musik City, Studio One, and D. Darling. Reggae music was about to be born.

6
BOB MARLEY AND THE BIRTH OF ROOTS REGGAE

Bob Marley, Wailer frontman, spokesman, alarming singer of equally alarming songs, is the Bob Dylan of reggae. He is cosmic mutant, sci-fi materialization of some futurist human being—wild and angry young man with tribulation on his mind. He has the Peace of Ras Tafari. . . . He is fly on the plastic wallpapers of Caribbean Society, exorcist for his people. He's been inside and outside the government yards and he shot the sheriff. —Idris Walters, Let It Rock, 1974[1]

ROBERT NESTA MARLEY WAS BORN ON FEBRUARY 6, 1945, in the rural parish of Nine Miles, St. Ann, a region with a rich history. Before the abolition of slavery in 1838, the plains of Nine Miles had sustained a stretch of rich sugarcane plantations, while small plots of land in the surrounding hills and mountains had been farmed by tenant slaves. Nesta, as he was called as a child, was the son of Cedella "Ciddy" Booker, a nineteen-year-old black woman, and Captain Norval Sinclair Marley, an older white man who had been a captain in the British army.

Nesta's grandfather, Omeriah Malcolm, was a man who had done well for himself. He owned a sizable house in the village of Nine Miles, prime cropland, a bakery, a grocery store, a dry-goods store, and a small coffee factory. He also was known as a *myalman*, a person who had the power to thwart obeah (sorcerer's magic) and to heal. It was in the course of business that Malcolm met Captain Norval Marley and introduced him to his daughter Ciddy, who was seventeen at the time. Captain Marley was superintendent for the Crown lands (British government–owned lands) in the area, and Ciddy was entranced by the dashing, romantic figure he cut in his uniform and on his horse. After seducing Ciddy, Captain Marley married her, but soon abandoned her, moving to Kingston, where he took another wife. Ciddy was left with an infant son to raise in her one-room hilltop shack near her father's home.

When Nesta was five years old, Captain Norval Marley wrote to Ciddy saying that he felt his son should be sent to him in Kingston. There, he said, Nesta could benefit from the better school system. Although reluctant to separate herself from her child, Ciddy realized how much such schooling could help Nesta. She made arrangements for him to be sent to Kingston, but to her cousin's house, not to Captain Marley's as she, understandably, did not completely trust him. When Nesta arrived in Kingston, however, Captain Marley was there to meet the bus and the Captain took Nesta away with him. Ciddy had no idea where Nesta was.

For nearly a year, Ciddy looked for word of her son from people traveling to and from Kingston. One day, finally, an acquaintance told her that she had seen Nesta in the Heywood section of the city. Ciddy immediately set out for Kingston, and after some searching, found Nesta in the care of a Miss Grey, who told Ciddy that Captain Marley had left the child with her the year before and never returned. Ciddy quickly packed up Nesta and his things and returned with him to the country.

For the next several years, Nesta bounced between his grandfather's home and that of Ciddy's sister, Amy, in Nine Miles. In order to earn a living, Ciddy had moved to Kingston to work. High-spirited by nature, Nesta always seemed to be in some kind of trouble, usually with his cousin Slegger, Amy's son. At last, fed up with the tricks and trouble of the two boys, Omeriah Marshall decided that Nesta belonged in Kingston with Ciddy. Ciddy was living in the Trench Town section of Kingston with Thaddeus (Toddy) Livingston and his son Bunny, who was two years younger than the ten-year-old Nesta. So Nesta went to Trench Town, which he would later immortalize in such poignant songs as "Trench Town Rock" and "No Woman No Cry." There he would put away his childhood name to become known as Bob Marley or, in the oppressive quarters of Trench Town, by his street name, Tuff Gong.

Years later, Marley said, "You look into my yard. It's a ghetto. This is ghetto you're looking at."[2] Trench Town in Kingston was a slum of shacks, rudies, and crime. To try to keep Marley from turning to a life of crime, Ciddy enrolled both him and Bunny Livingston in the Model Private School near Hanover Street. Marley didn't take to education, and by the time he was fourteen, he had left school and was training to be a welder. His real love was music, however, as it was for so many of the young men who lived in the ghettos of Kingston. He and Bunny Livingston (later known as Bunny Wailer) hung out at the record stores, listening to the latest hits, and joined the group who flocked to the Third Street house of musician Joe Higgs to learn to sing and play various instruments. Higgs had recorded a ska record with Roy Wilson, "Manny-O," in 1959 that had been wildly successful, selling

Bunny Wailer

thirty thousand copies. "Nesta was among those drawn to these get-togethers, bringing along Bunny [Wailer, and] Peter Tosh. . . ."³ Marley and the other boys viewed music not only as something that was fun and would garner attention, but as a way of getting out of the dead-end existence of the ghetto.

Marley wanted to make a record, be a star. He haunted Clement Dodd's record store, Musik City, and Dodd's recording studio, Federal Studios, hoping to get an audition with Dodd to make a record. One day outside the Federal Studios building, Marley encountered Leslie Kong, who had just opened his own recording studio. Kong had been recording a fourteen-year-old named James Chambers who would become almost as famous as Bob Marley under the name Jimmy Cliff. Kong asked Marley if he was there to audition, and when Marley said yes, had him sing right there in the street, without any instruments or backup. After a few bars of one of the songs Marley had composed, Kong told him he would record him, paying Marley £20 and giving him a copy of the demo record. His first records were "Judge Not" and "One Cup of Coffee," neither of which saw any success. Marley would record six other songs for Kong's Beverley Label, but eventually the two had a falling out, Marley claiming that Kong owed him money that was never paid for the last two songs he had recorded.

Marley continued to hang out with Bunny Livingston at Joe Higgs's home; there, the two met another young man, Peter Tosh (shortened from McIntosh). With the encouragement of Higgs, the three learned harmony, vocal control, and music theory, working together to sing as a group. Under the urging of Marley, the three formed a group, first called the Teenagers, then the Wailers. "Bob wanted the group . . . to have a full New Orleans–style vocal sound, so he asked two Rema girls, Beverly Kelso and Cherry Green, to sing backup. Another big-voiced boy, Junior Braithwaite, was added to share lead vocals with Bob."[4] After hearing the group practice and coaching them, Joe Higgs recom-

mended them to Clement "Coxsone" Dodd, for whom Higgs himself had begun recording. In December of 1962, the Wailers nervously auditioned at Dodd's studio.

Although the group was rough, Dodd felt they all had potential, particularly Bob Marley, and signed them to a contract that gave him exclusive rights to their

Bob Marley and the Wailers in Jamaica, 197

records and making him their manager. In return, the Wailers would earn £20 for each side they recorded. Although this sounds as if Dodd were taking advantage of the four young men, there were many others just waiting in line for such a deal, hoping to make it big. Recording was one of the few ways out of the ghettos of Kingston, one of the few ways to make a name for oneself.

The day after the signing, the Wailers made their first recording, three ska songs: "Simmer Down," "I Am Going Home," and "Do You Remember." The recording seemed in many ways to be amateurish, the singing nervous, but Dodd felt the group had something and he released "Simmer Down," a ska song that dealt with rudie concerns, in December 1963. Within a few days of its release, it was already garnering an audience. There was something in the music that listeners liked—and wanted more of. After this modest success, Dodd brought in experienced studio musicians to back them up—including virtuoso pianist Jackie Mittoo of the Skatalites, who had established not only the basic rhythms associated with ska, but would lay down those that later flowed beneath reggae, dancehall, and ragga. In addition, Dodd hired Tommy McCook on tenor sax, Jah Jerry on guitars, and Hugh Malcolm on drums, among others.

With this backing, the Wailers recorded a number

of sides, and rerecorded "Simmer Down," which went Number 1 on the Jamaican charts in February 1964. This was followed by the success of "It Hurts to Be Alone," featuring Junior Braithwaite as lead singer, and "Lonesome Feeling," with lead vocal by Bunny Wailer. Between 1963 and 1966, the Wailers recorded more than seventy songs for Dodd, of which twenty or more became hits.

Dodd had first seen the Wailers as just another slick R & B or ska group, but with the success of "Simmer Down," it became evident that they were much more. The Wailers weren't just crooning love songs, they were experimenting with various styles of music, from U.S. soul to rudie sounds, singing about the life they knew in the ghettos of Kingston. And what they sang captivated young Jamaican audiences. Early on, Dodd decided to push the Wailers and bought stage outfits of cheap gold lamé for the group, entered them in some talent contests, and arranged for some live appearances.

In September of 1964, the Wailers lost Junior Braithwaite, who left the group and moved to Chicago, hoping to pursue a career in medicine. (He did not return to Jamaica until 1984, when Bunny Wailer asked him to participate in a recording project, "Never Ending Wailers," an album released in 1991 that combined old tracks of Bob Marley singing with new tracks done by Bunny,

Junior, Peter Tosh, and Constantine "Vision" Walker, a later addition to the Wailers. Braithwaite died on June 2, 1999, murdered in the home of a friend in Kingston, Jamaica.)

By 1964, the Wailers were dominating ska music in Jamaica, and ska was spreading to the United States and Great Britain. Chris Blackwell and his Island Records had scored a hit with Millie Small's "My Boy Lollipop," and the Jamaican government had featured her and a variety of other singers, including Cecil "Prince Buster" Campbell and Jimmy Cliff, at the Jamaican pavilion of the 1964 World's Fair in New York City. *Life* magazine had printed a picture of ska dancers and U.S. dance shows were teaching teenagers to do the steps. But the Wailers were not part of this spread of ska beyond the island. Ghetto violence had erupted at the Wailers' 1964 Christmas show in Kingston, putting the Wailers in disgrace with both the government and the police. For this reason, the government had not included them with the Jamaican delegation to the World's Fair; they were viewed as rudies, part of the undesirable element of Jamaican society. Nor were the Skatalites included, as most of them were Rastafarians and smoked ganja. Ever aware of Jamaica's public image and the need to draw tourists, the government ignored these aspects of island life.

On February 10, 1966, Marley married Rita Anderson, who then was a member of the girl group, the Soulettes. Rita had had her own hit, a version of the U.S. pop song "Pied Piper." Only ten days after their wedding, Marley left for Wilmington, Delaware, where his mother was living, to try to build a life away from Trench Town for his family. Ciddy had moved to Wilmington in 1962, with her daughter by Toddy Livingston, to seek new opportunities, and to be close to her sister Ivy Brown, who also lived there. She had been urging

Marley to come to the States for some time, and after his marriage, he decided the time was right. He found, however, that opportunities were limited for someone with his educational level and skills. Rita and their daughter Sharon joined him in August of 1966, but Marley promptly sent her home. He had lost his job and found he was eligible to be drafted into the U.S.

Rita Marley

Army, and in October he returned to Jamaica.

Earlier, in April of 1966, the Emperor Haile Selassie had visited the island. For the Rastafarians living in Jamaica, this visit was the equivalent of a visit from the Messiah. Rita Marley was present to see his motorcade go by and was drawn to him. Although she had been mistrustful and fearful of Rastafarians previously, seeing Haile Selassie converted her to Rastafarianism and she immediately wrote to her husband, who was still in the United States, telling him of her experience, which she saw as a revelation. When Marley returned to the island, he, too, was drawn to Rastafarianism, at first reluctantly. After speaking at length with Rita, and with Mortimo Planno of the the Divine Theocratic Temple of Rastafari in Kingston, Marley was won over, as were the other members of the Wailers, and soon all three began to grow their hair out into dreads and live according to Rasta beliefs.

Marley had returned to Jamaica with his savings, intending to start his own recording company. He began the Wail 'N Soul 'M record label (named for the Wailers and Rita's Marley's group, the Soulettes), and Rita and Marley opened a record store, the Soul Shack. Although the Wailers recorded a number of songs for Wail 'N Soul 'M, including "Nice Time," "Thank You Lord," and "Pyaka," the label did not have the kind of distribution that older, more established labels did, and the business finally failed.

The Wailers also entered into an agreement with the African American singer Johnny Nash to earn some money. Marley was signed by Nash and his manager Danny Sims, to be a songwriter, while the Wailers were put on retainer to make demo records for them. In 1972, Nash would break the charts in Great Britain with Marley's "Stir It Up." The Wailers, now a trio consisting of Marley, Peter Tosh, and Bunny Wailer, also began recording again—this time playing rock steady, with its slower beat—for both Dodd, and for Leslie Kong (with a hiatus during 1967 to 1968 while Bunny Wailer served a one-year, two-month sentence for marijuana possession, and in 1969, when Marley returned to the United States, where he worked on the assembly line at the Chrysler plant in Wilmington to earn badly needed money). As with Marley's earlier association with Kong, this later alliance meant bad news for Marley and the Wailers. The songs recorded for him did not sell well, and the association with Kong had alienated Dodd. The Wailers began looking for a new label.

Kong and others, however, were starting to promote a new sort of music, different from the rock steady that the Wailers were producing. In 1968, Kong released the Maytals' "Do the Reggay," the first record to use the term *reggae*. Dodd's Studio One, meanwhile, was distributing Larry and Alvin's "Nanny Goat," and producer Harry Johnson had recorded the Beltones' "No More Heartaches," both of which had the distinctive reggae beat and lyrics. Roots reggae, with its reliance on burru drumming and themes of political protest, was quickly becoming the music of the day. "Reggae in all its variations signaled a break from the smoothness of rock steady and the aspirations . . . to replicate the refinement of Detroit and Chicago soul."[5]

Lee "Scratch" Perry was a record producer who had previously worked for Dodd. He had been born in Kendal, Jamaica, in 1936, and when he arrived in Kingston in the late 1950s, immediately wanted to get into the music business. He first worked for Coxsone Dodd, but left after a disagreement over money. He then worked for the Amalgamated label of producer Joel Gibson, where he recorded an early reggae hit, "People Funny Boy," and then began his own

Peter Tosh

Upsetters Record label. Perry, through luck or chance, had picked up on the music that was going to replace rock steady. His Upsetters Record studio band with its quicker reggae rhythms had produced a hit in 1969, "Return of Django," that resulted in a six-week tour of Britain for the band. When the Upsetters band returned from England, Bob Marley approached them about backing up the Wailers, and they agreed. Perry was upset, thinking they were leaving his studio, but worked out an agreement with Marley and the Wailers to produce their work.

In the ska and rock steady songs of the Wailers composed by Bob Marley, he had incorporated some of his feelings about rudies and Trench Town. Now, fueled by his Rasta beliefs and the evocative beats of reggae, Marley's music blossomed into maturity. Reggae was the vehicle through which Marley could fully express himself, his hopes and beliefs, and by extension, the hopes and beliefs of the underprivileged worldwide. It was a music ideally suited to him. As Toots Hibbert of Toots and the Maytals said, "Reggae means coming from the people, you know? . . . Reggae means *regular* people who are suffering, and don't have what they want."[6] In 1976, Marley affirmed this, saying, "My music fights against the system that teaches to live and die."[7] When Marley found his music—reggae—that suffering found a voice.

Although Leslie Kong was still issuing some of the Wailers' sides, Marley and the Wailers were doing most of their recording with Perry under the Wailers' Tuff Gong label. With Perry's encouragement and backing from the Upsetters (or the Hippy Boys, as they sometimes called themselves), the Wailers, and Marley in particular, flourished, experimenting with lyrics, instrumentation, and incorporating elements of other types of music—jazz, gospel, rock—into their reggae songs. Critics often say that the songs that Marley and the Wailers produced for Perry are some of their best: "Duppy Conqueror," "Lively Up Yourself," "Small Axe," and others. The albums Perry produced with these songs were hugely popular: *Soul Rebels* (1970), *Soul Revolution I* (1970), and *Soul Revolution II* (1971). *Soul Rebels* was reissued in 1973 under the title *African Herbsman*, and *Soul Revolution I* was reissued in 1974 under the title *Rasta Revolution*.

Johnny Nash's manager, Danny Sims, set up negotiations for the Wailers with Nash's British label, CBS, in 1971, flying the Wailers to England. The Wailers recorded one of Marley's songs for CBS, "Reggae on Broadway," but it was a flop. Sims and Nash then left for the United States, leaving the Wailers stranded in England with no money, no plane fare back to Jamaica, and no contract. Desperate for anything, Marley marched into the offices of Chris Blackwell of Island records and demanded an interview.

Blackwell had been looking into the reggae scene in Jamaica and was interested, despite the fact that many in England felt that reggae was "noise fit only for cretinous skinheads," and music only for the ghetto.[8] In 1972, the Wailers signed a contract with Blackwell, who provided the group's airfare back to Jamaica, and later gave Marley a mansion in Kingston in which to live.

In 1973, the Wailers' first album for Island, *Catch a Fire*, was released. At first, it only sold moderately well, but after the Wailers toured England to promote it, sales began to soar, and at the end of the year, they recorded their second Island album, *Burnin'*. In 1974, rocker Eric Clapton had recorded Marley's "I Shot the Sheriff," which became an international hit and brought even more attention to the Wailers.

Although *Catch a Fire* continued to sell steadily, *Burnin'* brought the Wailers to the world's attention. The cover featured a picture of Marley, complete with dreadlocks, sucking on a huge spliff; inside were pictures of Kingston ghetto life, its shantys and poverty. The album seemed dangerous to many, and the American press published a number of articles both on Marley and the Wailers, and on Rastafarianism which, until this time, had largely gone ignored outside Jamaica. Reggae and Rastafarianism got an additional boost in the United States with the 1972 release of singer Jimmy Cliff's film *The Harder They Come*, a film in which Blackwell also had a small investment. When they went on tour as the opening act during 1973 for Sly and the Family Stone, the Wailers began to receive so much press that, after five performances, Sly fired them; he didn't like the attention being taken away from his own group.

With the Wailers' success, Blackwell wanted the group touring more, promoting their work, but neither Bunny Wailer nor Peter Tosh wanted to travel. Chris Blackwell said, "Peter was always difficult. I found Bunny easier than him, because Bunny was consistently no: he didn't want to tour overseas, he didn't want to do this, do that, didn't want to have anything to do with Babylon. Peter was yes and then no, yes and then no. And that was more difficult."[9] Bunny Wailer refused to tour. Peter Tosh not only didn't like touring, but was resentful of the attention that Bob Marley received; the Wailers, after all, was supposed to be a group, with no one person more important than another. Finally, both Bunny Wailer and Tosh quit the group. Bunny Wailer continues to promote the Wailers' music. Tosh's solo career ended when he was murdered in his Barbican, St. Andrew home in Jamaica by an unknown gunman in 1987.

To emphasize the change, Marley changed the group's name from the Wailers to Bob Marley and the Wailers. By 1974, Marley had a new agent, Don Taylor, and was backed by a top-notch group of Jamaican musicians and I-Three, a female harmony group consisting of Marley's wife, Rita, Marcia Griffiths, and Judy Mowatt. The next album, *Natty Dread*, caused problems in Jamaica for Tosh. One song, "Revolution," was interpreted by the Jamaican Labour Party as calling for revolution. Although no longer with Marley and the Wailers, Tosh was beaten by the police as an example to the group.

By 1976, Bob Marley and the Wailers were touring the world, but politics was heating up in Jamaica. That year, Marley agreed to perform at a concert in Kingston's National Heroes Park. Although the concert was intended to bring the two opposing political parties—the Jamaican Labour Party (JLP) and the People's National Party (PNP)—together, many saw it as a ploy by the People's National Party to promote the agenda of Prime Minister Michael Manley. As Marley's manager Don Taylor said, "Between the political factions among us, a yawning gulf had opened."[10] The lid blew off two days before the concert when gunmen burst into Marley's Kingston home, spraying the room with bullets. Marley was shot in the arm and nicked

Bob Marley in performance with I-Three, his backup singers, in 1974

in the chest; Rita Marley was grazed in the head; a friend, Lewis Griffith was wounded; and Don Taylor suffered a near-fatal shot in the back. Despite his minor injuries, Marley decided to go ahead with the concert. It was more important than ever, he felt, to try to bring Jamaicans together, to try to stop such brutality.

Although Bob and Rita Marley left Jamaica soon after the concert, moving to London to work on the next album, *Exodus*, bad luck seemed to follow them. In the spring of 1977, Marley and one of the Wailers' musicians, bassist Aston Barrett, were arrested in London and fined for possession of marijuana. In September, while in Miami, Florida, Marley was diagnosed with a cancerous growth on his toe from an injury he had received earlier in 1972 while playing soccer, a sport he loved.

Over the next eight years, Marley recorded four albums—*Kaya* and *Babylon by Bus* (1978), *Survival* (1979), and *Uprising* (1980)—and toured in England, Europe, and Africa, where he garnered a huge following. But his health was beginning to deteriorate. In September of 1980, while in New York to perform at Madison Square Garden, Marley collapsed while jogging in Central Park. When he was examined, doctors found that the cancer that had originally been in his toe had spread to other parts of his body. In November, after his conversion to Ethiopian Orthodox Christianity, a faith adhered to by one group within Rastafarianism, he traveled to Bavaria to the clinic of Dr. Josef Issels, who was known for his unorthodox nontoxic cancer treatments. After five months, however, Dr. Issels released him so that he could go home to Miami where his mother, now Cedella Booker, lived; the cancer had spread to Marley's brain and there was nothing further Issels could do.

On May 11, 1981, Bob Marley died at the Cedars of Lebanon Hospital only a month after he had been awarded Jamaica's third-highest civil honor, the Order of Merit. Mourned by all of Jamaica, his body lay in state in the National Heroes Arena in Kingston, and then was buried at his birthplace of Nine Miles on May 21, carried there in a funeral procession that stretched more than fifty miles.

Upon hearing of Marley's death, fans and friends throughout the world mourned. Chris Blackwell said, "I can say nothing other than that it's a terrible, awful loss. Bob's career was always much larger than music—and there was much more to come."[11]

In January of 1994, Bob Marley was inducted into the Rock and Roll Hall of Fame, but his fame had been assured long before that. Marley's records continue to be issued and to be popular, to move people; they are now considered classics. Although there were numerous other talented reggae musicians, none captured the hearts and minds of people around the world as Bob Marley did. To many, Bob Marley *was* and still *is* reggae music. Each year, Jamaica celebrates a February 6 Bob Marley Birthday Bash at Nine Miles, St. Ann, with performances by outstanding reggae artists. Included are appearances by Marley's children, who, since Marley's death, have formed the group the Melody Makers, and who continue to further the tradition of reggae.

Marley's death did not mean the end of reggae, or of his own brand of music. As he himself said in 1975, "My music will go on forever. Maybe it's a fool say that, but when me know facts me can say facts. My music go on forever."[12] And Marley's music has.

Ziggy Marley

As Judy Mowatt, a member of I-Three, said,

His music has caused people all over the universe to be enlightened, to be happy, to be dancing. . . . So I would just look at it that his spirit is really dancing, touching all nationalities. . . . He is not gone, man; his work is here. He is alive.[13]

7
BEYOND THE WAILERS

We have many special musicians in this town.
Let them be delivered as individuals.

—Prince Tony, U Roy Producer, 1976[1]

WHILE THE LEGEND OF BOB MARLEY SOARED beyond the shore of the island of Jamaica to circle the world and become inextricably linked with reggae, he was not alone in following the music's beat. Before Marley had ventured into reggae, Toots Hibbert and the Maytals, who had introduced the word *reggae* with their 1968 "Do the Reggay," had followed this hit up with many others. During the 1980s and '90s, Toots and the Maytals inspired fans around the world, although earlier, their fame and popularity had been limited primarily to Jamaica. According to critic Colin Larkin, the Maytals were only kept from becoming "international" artists by the runaway success of Bob Marley and The Wailers in the '70s. Rumour has it that Island Records' Chris Blackwell originally only signed the Wailers because he was unable to obtain the Maytals' signatures at the time.[2]

Frederick "Toots" Hibbert was born in May Pen, Clarendon, in 1946. While growing up, he displayed an early talent for music, singing with his brothers and sisters at services in the local Baptist church. Like so many young Jamaican men in the late 1950s, Hibbert moved to Kingston to seek his fortune. For a time, he worked in a barbershop. Hibbert was accustomed to singing while he worked and his talent drew the attention of two other young men, Henry "Raleigh" Gordon, and Nathaniel "Jerry" Mathias. The three decided to form a group; Raleigh Gordon came up with the name, the Maytals.

Ska was hot. Hibbert intended the Maytals to be the hottest ska group in Jamaica, and it did seem as if his dream would come true. The group seemed magical and were soon recording for Coxsone Dodd's Studio One. Even in his early records, Hibbert connected music and religion. His first side for Studio One, "Hallelujah," "set a scorching pace, harnessing an 'old time religion' feel to the powerful new ska beat."[3] Later, while recording for Prince Buster, Hibbert incorporated both the rhythms and messages of Rastafarianism into his music.

Toots and the Maytals nearly missed the rock steady era of Jamaican music. In 1966, the group won the Jamaican Festival Song Competition, a prestigious contest, with their "Bam Bam," aimed at rudies. But, from 1966 to 1968, Hibbert was in prison for possession of marijuana. After his release in 1968, Toots and the Maytals hit the charts with the rudie rock steady tune, "54-46 That's My Number," titled for Hibbert's prison number.

Reggae rhythms, however, were beginning to fill the air and Hibbert quickly capitalized on their popularity with his "Do the Reggay." From the time they began recording, the group skillfully adapted to each change in music, and with each change, had moved to the number-one spot on the Jamaican charts. The same happened when Hibbert and the Maytals began producing reggae songs. Even in 1975, however, the only Toots and the Maytals' recordings in the United States were two tracks for Jimmy Cliff's film, *The Harder They Come*. For all their talent, the group was only locally known, although the potential for greater fame was evident.

Toots and the Maytals' reggae, usually backed by a studio band, was rough and powerful. In 1977, Lester Bangs of *Stereo Review* said of Hibbert,

> With his deep, groaning, bluesy voice and the relentlessly churning arrangements that support it, Toots Hibbert and the Maytals should be instantly relevant to anyone who grew up on American soul music of the sixties. . . . His music rocks more solidly than just about anyone else's in reggae. . . . Toots' songs have a universality that many of his peers' odes to Jah Rastafari fall far short of. . . . [4]

Many of Hibbert's early songs are assured a place in Jamaican musical history: the driving "Bam Bam"; "Monkey Man," which made it onto the British charts; and 1969's "Sweet and Dandy." During the 1980s and '90s, Toots and the Maytals at last achieved an international reputation, touring in both England and the United States. Currently, Hibbert sometimes tours without the Maytals, and as he has done throughout his musical career, continues to experiment with his music and lyrics, most recently trying out some nonreggae arrangements while on tour.

Just as Toots and the Maytals preceded and set the stage for the meteoric rise of Bob Marley, Jimmy Cliff popularized reggae in film and brought it to the attention of both British and U.S. fans, paving the way for Marley and the Wailers. As Cliff said in a 1981 *Rolling Stone* interview:

> I've been doing what I had to do, which is like a shepherd's work within the reggae idiom. The shepherd is the one who opens the gate. That has always been my part, you know, to make the way.[5]

Jimmy Cliff was born James Chambers in St. Catherine, Jamaica, in 1948, and moved to Kingston to go to school in 1962. Lured by the booming record industry, he began recording for a number of smaller sound systems when he was only fourteen years old, making a minor splash with such sides as "Daisy Got Me Crazy," for Count Boysie, and "I'm Sorry," for Sir Cavalier. Although these were well received, Cliff didn't gain wide public attention until he recorded a song he had written himself, "Hurricane Hattie," about a recent hurricane that had decimated the Caribbean. It quickly became an island hit and brought him to the attention of Leslie Kong, who recorded Cliff's ska hits, "King of Kings" and "Dearest Beverly" in 1963. These, plus a tour with Bryon Lee and the Dragonaires, sponsored by politician Edward Seaga, a tour designed to publicize Jamaican music beyond Jamaica, caused Cliff to be noticed by Island Records' Chris Blackwell.

Blackwell signed Cliff, moved him to England, and began to promote him aggressively. In 1968, Cliff competed in the International Song Festival in Brazil and his song "Waterfall" earned him a substantial South American following. A later tour to a number of countries in Africa broadened Cliff's fan base, and in Britain, Cliff finally gained fame with his 1969 "Wonderful World, Beautiful People." In the United States, Cliff struck a similar cord with his "Vietnam." This song earned him the praise of both Bob Dylan and Paul Simon, and inspired the latter in the making of his "Mother and Child Reunion." All the while, Cliff's music was developing, moving from ska to roots reggae. It wasn't until the 1972 film *The Harder They Come*, however, that Cliff fully embraced roots reggae with enthusiasm:

> Cliff, with his ever-present five-point star T-shirt, was suddenly Jamaica's most marketable property. *The Harder They Come* was the island's best homegrown film, and its soundtrack one of the biggest-selling reggae records of all time.[6]

The film, now on video, went on to become something of a cult classic, but Cliff, who had seemed to be on his way to explosive, international fame, inexplicably faded into the background of the reggae scene, eclipsed by Bob Marley and the Wailers. When asked what had happened, Cliff said in an interview,

> I changed. I went into a heavy spiritual and cultural thing, which I felt was more important. I still made records, but my interest wasn't a hundred percent into the music. But by about 1977 . . . I started seriously getting back into music.[7]

Although still a huge star in South America and Africa, Cliff only recently emerged from his self-imposed exile from actively performing, when his song, "Many Rivers to Cross" became an enormous hit for the new roots reggae group UB40.

Equally overshadowed by the success of Bob Marley, at least in the United States, was Marley's producer, Lee "Scratch" Perry, who was and is himself a talented, although eccentric, singer and songwriter. Temperamental, and as Marley called him, a "genius," Perry was born Rainford Hugh Perry, in 1936, in Hanover, Jamaica. When he came to Kingston in the 1950s, Perry began his career in music with Coxsone Dodd, with whom he had a falling-out in the 1960s. At the same time, he was recording other groups for Dodd, Perry also began releasing his own records:

> Featuring a bluesy, declamatory vocal style over superb backing from the legendary Skatalites, these tracks set a pattern from which Perry . . . rarely deviated. Social and personal justice, bawdy, sometimes lewd, sexual commentary, and . . . stinging attacks on musical rivals . . . are all prefigured on these early tracks such as "Prince in The Pack," Trial And Crosses," "Help The Weak," "Give Me Justice," "Chicken Scratch" (from which he acquired his nickname), "Doctor Dick" with Rita Marley and the Soulettes on backing vocals, and "Madhead," recorded between 1963 and 1966.[8]

Although his records met with success, Perry found himself occupied more and more with the recording of other artists, particularly after he began producing under his own Upsetter label, and later, established his own studio, Black Ark. The records that he produced featured not only the Wailers, but also such singers and groups as David Isaacs, the Untouchables, Val Bennett, Dave Barker (Dave and Ansell Collins), Junior Byles, and other legends of reggae. In many ways, the records produced by Perry comprise the bulk of roots reggae greats.

During the late 1970s, while he continued to produce, Perry began experimenting with recording artists featuring different styles of music, moving away from the roots reggae that had built both his name and his studio. As a result, the success that had followed him disappeared; the records Black Ark was putting out were barely noticed. Faced with this downturn, Perry's behavior became odd and erratic, and in 1980, he trashed and burned his Black Ark studio and fled, first to Britain, then to Holland. After recording a number of solo albums that were far removed from the reggae that had been so successful for him, in 1990, he married a wealthy Swiss woman and returned to Jamaica. Although Perry has yet to find himself musically in the new millennium, he did produce one stellar collection of artists from his Black Ark days: Arkology, which, as Colin Larkin points out, "presents some of the most vital music ever to have come from Jamaica."[9]

Another who has undertaken the task of preserving some of the classics of reggae, as well as producing his own music, is former Wailer, Bunny Livingston (Wailer). The only surviving Wailer, Bunny Livingston was born Neville O'Riley Livingston in Kingston in 1947. When Cedella Marley moved to Kingston to live with Livingston's father, Toddy, Livingston found a brother and good friend in Bob Marley. Both boys were captured by the musical revolution then sweeping Kingston and when the Wailers were formed, Livingston's high tenor became a key ingredient in their harmony. Occasionally, his voice was featured in such early Wailers' songs as "Dancing Shoes," and "He Who Feels It Knows It." In 1968, after spending some time in prison for alleged marijuana possession, despite the fact that arresting officers had found none on him, Livingston wrote the song "Battering Down Sentence," which was later featured on his solo album *Blackheart Man*, released in 1976, the title track of which is considered a masterpiece in reggae music.

As the Wailers grew in popularity and fame, there was increasing pressure on the group to do more touring, something Livingston hated. There was also increasing dissension within the group. Peter Tosh, the third Wailer, felt that Marley was taking over the group with Chris Blackwell's blessing, overshadowing him and Livingston. As Carl Gayle said,

> It became obvious to Island pretty soon that Marley was the one to pin the genius tag on. Bob, with his rebel rasta image, was projected as the key figure to the exclusion of Tosh and Livingston[10]

When Tosh departed the Wailers in 1974, it seemed like a good time for Livingston to leave also and to pursue a solo career, setting up his own Solomonic label in Kingston. Unlike Tosh, Livingston remained on good terms with Marley until Marley's death in 1981.

While still with the Wailers, Livingston had tested the solo waters with the release of a single, "Searching for Love," that had met with moderate success. In 1975, his Solomonic label produced his "Life Line," "Bide Up," "Pass It On," and "Arabs Oil Weapon," and in 1976, Island records distributed *Blackheart Man*. This was followed by quite a number of other singles, and three albums (*Protest*, 1977; *Struggle*, 1979; *In I Father's House*, 1980).

After the release of his 1980 album, Livingston, who by now had long been known as Bunny Wailer, turned to producing various "tribute" records to Bob Marley. This led to dissension and legal problems with Marley's heirs: Marley's mother, his wife, Rita, and his children. Livingston also tried his hand at recording in the new styles that had begun to sweep Jamaica during the 1980s and '90s, dub and dance-hall; this proved rather disastrous. In December of 1990, when he appeared at the Reggae Sting concert, audience members drove him from the stage under a hail of bottles. Livingston upbraided them for "disrespecting dem own reggae king."[11] Three years later, when Livingston released his single, "Woman," *Beat* magazine damned it in one word: "Awful."[12] Since that time, Livingston has relied on his royalties from Wailers' albums, and has himself returned to reggae.

Despite his more recent failures, Livingston is

assured a place in a reggae hall of fame not only from his work with Marley and the Wailers, but for many of his own solo songs and albums. In addition to his substantial body of work in reggae, his dance-hall classic, "Cool Runnings," of 1981, heralded a shift from the more militant reggae that spoke of revolution and a return to Africa, to lyrics that, instead, praise the possibility of a better life in this world.

Toots and the Maytals, Jimmy Cliff, Lee "Scratch" Perry, and Bunny Livingston are only four of the thousands of talented musicians who recorded during the "golden" years of reggae music in Jamaica, and who continue to work within the style. While Bob Marley brought reggae to the world, in many ways, he also inadvertently did a disservice to the music by overshadowing the many other artists who were and are also deserving of recognition.

8
NEW WAVES IN JAMAICA: DUB, DANCEHALL, AND RAGGA

Dub music is like a long echo looping through time. . . .
Spreading out a song or a groove over a vast landscape of
peaks and deep trenches, extending hooks and beats to
vanishing point, dub creates new maps of time, intangible
sound sculptures, sacred sites, balm and shock for mind,
body, and spirit.
—David Toop, 1995[1]

EVEN AS ROOTS REGGAE WAS SWEEPING THE HILLS
and cities of Jamaica and flowing out into the world,
artists were experimenting and changing it, developing new music. Three styles that still have followers and which grew from advances in recording
technology are dub, dancehall, and ragga.

Originally, during the birth of the sound systems,
a *dub* meant a recording made specifically for DJs to
use, but during the late 1960s the word came to

include the technique known as remixing:

> These re-mixes radically manipulate and reshape the recording (through the use of sound effects). The production and mixing process is not used just to replicate the live performance of the recording artist, but audio effects and studio 'trickery' are seen as an integral part of the music.[2]

At first, dub versions of popular reggae songs consisted entirely of the instrumental track of that song with the vocals removed, and were made to be used by sound systems. More and more, however, audiences hearing the dub records wanted copies, so the various recording studios began issuing them for sale. As the studio engineers began experimenting with the tracks, however, the music became a hit in itself and a dub version of a song was often issued as the B side of a record. Just as each sound-system owner vied with other owners to have the best and newest records, as dub caught on, the owners also wanted more original dub versions, and one man in particular was able to supply these.

Osbourne Ruddock, known as "King Tubby," was born in Kingston in 1941, and became an electronics engineer working both for his own sound system, Home Town Hi-Fi, and for Duke Reid at Treasure Island Studio. King Tubby was truly king in the art of remixing, adding his own echo and reverb effects, and is credited with inventing dub music. His dub records were so hot that by 1972, working with his friend, Bunny "Striker" Lee, his own sound system was the most popular on the music scene, and his dub versions of hit records were the ones that listeners wanted the most. Steve Barrow notes, "Improvisation was the order of the day; most of Tubby's dubs were mixed live, with the engineer playing his board like a great jazzman blowing solos on his horn, deconstructing and reinventing the music."[3]

With King Tubby's success mixing dub records, others began to ask him to show them how to do what he did. King Tubby wound up hiring and training some of the best remixers of the decade: "Prince" Philip Smart, Lloyd "Prince Jammy" James, and Overton "Scientist" Brown. James was the first hired by King Tubby as his dub engineer, and in 1978, founded his own label, "Imprint."

About the same time that King Tubby was finding success with his dub versions of songs, he began working with a local DJ, Edwart Beckford, who was also known as U-Roy. In DJ-ing records, like Count Machuki earlier, U-Roy had begun to add his own jive talk, toasting and rapping between records and while the record was playing. King Tubby recognized U-Roy's talent and recommended him for

Duke Reid's system. As King Tubby said, "An I'm get U-Roy—that time, firs' time at the dance hall, you only hear—like, a deejay would be talkin' on a record—it's not really a rhythm, the record would be singin' and part of the introduction of the record, the deejay would talk. But U-Roy come in an' mek it a splash, man, an' I couldn't do nothing wrong for Duke Reid."[4] U-Roy recorded his dub raps for Duke Reid with great success. His first, "Wake the Town," a dub version of "Girl I've Got a Date," by Alton Ellis, quickly rose to the number-one spot on Jamaica's radio charts, and later his versions of other songs proved to be equal hits.

Of course, U-Roy's successful jive techniques were soon being copied by other DJs and MCs working for competing sound systems and record labels, and the practice of toasting and rapping grew beyond the shores of Jamaica, moving to America and forming the basis of the rap music of the 1970s and after. In Great Britain, the style evolved into Trip Hop, Drum and Bass, and Jungle—all versions of Jamaican dub and American rap. One of the leading producers of British dub, Adrian Sherwood, like King Tubby, took remixing beyond merely eliminating the vocals of a song. "Often wildly experimental with studio techniques, sometimes running whole tracks in reverse, [he] has also attracted artists from outside the realm of 'dub' such as Depeche Mode,

Nine Inch Nails, Living Color, Garbage, and The Cure, all of who[m] have used Sherwood's radical approach to mixing to manipulate their material."[5]

The popularity of dub records led to the release of dub albums. The first Jamaican album, recorded in 1973, was Lee "Scratch" Perry's *Blackboard Jungle Dub*, mixed by King Tubby himself. Producers in England quickly jumped on the bandwagon with Keith Hudson's *Pick A Dub* (1974) as the first British album. By the mid-'70s, dub of all kinds, including "roots" dub made from roots reggae records, had taken over the airwaves. By 1982, however, dub had morphed into rap in the United States and Trip Hop in Great Britain, while the original dub style of King Tubby continued to exist in their shadows. In 1995 Marc Weidenbaum reported in *Pulse!* that a dub revival was occurring in the United States, particularly on the West Coast, with such groups as Dub Narcotic Sound System and President's Breakfast, which were "using dub as a creative launchpad."[6] "What's apparent," Weidenbaum wrote, "is that dub has become the reigning metaphor for reconciling the tradition of live musical performance . . . with the abstract art of using the studio as a recording instrument. . . . The reverberating waves of their sound systems have grown wider and more far-reaching, only to encompass the most creative pop music of our day."[7]

In Jamaica in the early 1980s, two related musical innovations were emerging, dancehall, and ragga. Dancehall earned its name because it was made to meet the need for music to dance to in the Jamaican dance halls. Although the roots reggae of Bob Marley and other musicians had been hugely popular, it was not music that could be danced to. Dancehall "first emerged at the start of the '80s and was so called because it began in the dances that have always been the lifeblood of Jamaican music . . . dancehall was the least fanciful genre of reggae to date, offering the rhythm, a voice, the dancers' energy and little else."[8] Dancehall initially used dub versions of records that stressed the rhythms of the original song, with DJs or MCs talking or chanting along with them, in essence creating a merger between reggae and rap. But as dancehall caught on, groups began recording original records and albums to fill the need. Unlike reggae, however, dancehall was more hedonistic and tended not to dabble heavily in universal social issues; "Now the emphasis shifted to traditional dancehall concerns—new dance moves, slackness (sexually explicit lyrics), and sound clashes."[9]

Dancehall reflected the changing priorities of Jamaicans. "After [Bob] Marley died," Guy Garcia wrote in *Time* in 1993, "a new generation of Trench

Town youths began to forge a harder, denser style of reggae called dancehall. Reflecting the desperate times in Kingston's ghettos, dancehall lyrics were charged with angry diatribes glorifying guns, drugs, and sex, and sung often in a fast, talky style called 'toasting.'"[10] Whereas roots reggae singers, such as Marley, incorporated their Rastafarian beliefs and messages of hope into their music, dancehall was more insular, reflecting the immediate concerns of islanders. While roots reggae was global, universal, dancehall focused on "microrealities, the obsessive minutiae of Jamaican urban life which holds little meaning for all outsiders."[11]

This concern with island life emerged from the violence and political upheaval in Jamaica in the 1970s and '80s, the same struggle that had precipitated the shooting of Bob Marley before his "One Love Peace Concert" in 1972. Unlike Marley, however, the response by this new breed of musicians, as Louis Chude-Sokei points out, was "not to accept themselves as passive victims in an overwhelming Babylonian structure, not to represent themselves as 'wailers,' as victims of history belonging to a helplessly innocent race. . . . This can be seen in the incredible boasting and self-assertions that are typical of dancehall and the 'fearless' rudeboys. . . . Instead, they see themselves in many ways as being free within Babylon to destroy history and rebuild community. . . ."[12]

During the 1980s, a number of singers and groups emerged who specialized in dancehall music: Yellowman, an albino MC; Barrington Levy; and General Echo. Even Bunny Livingston, backed by the dancehall band the Roots Radics, tried his hand at dancehall with his popular "Cool Runnings" in 1981. Many of these artists had releases in Great Britain, where dancehall also had and still has a strong following. Even as late as 1985, King Jammy's "Under Me Sleng Deng," produced in the digitally synthesized style of dancehall called "ragga-muffin" or "ragga," topped the charts. Because of its rhythmic appeal and danceability, dancehall continues to be popular both on the island of Jamaica and abroad, with such artists as Elephant Man, Mr. Vegas, Cobra, Baby Doll, Lady Saw, Spragga Benz, Zebra, Scare Dem Crew, and of course, the current king of dancehall/ragga, Beenie Man.

"Ragga is . . . barely distinguishable from the earlier dancehall, the main differences being its slightly more aggressive attitude, an alignment with the concerns of its youthful audience—one-upmanship, guns, sex—and an all-important, rocking electronic beat."[13] The main differences between dancehall and ragga are the use of current technology to create the music, and a shift to lyrics that celebrate gun violence, and to "slack" (sexually explicit) lyrics that

hark back to the tradition of
mento. "Mento music, which
shares elements of the Trinidadian
calypso, particularly the penchant
for sexual double entendre, is an
undisputed progenitor of contem-
porary ragga/dancehall music."[14]
Ragga lyrics often glamorize sex
and violence, and many critics
have railed against them, particularly in the unstable social and
political environment of Jamaica

Yellowman

in the 1980s. The 1990s, however, saw a subtle shift
in emphasis in the lyrics of ragga, toward a greater
sense of social consciousness and spirituality. Credit
for this is often laid at the doorstep of ragga artist
Buju Banton (Mark Anthony Myrie).

Buju Banton was born in Kingston, and began
DJing when he was fifteen years old with the Roots
Unlimited sound system, and recording for DJ Red
Dragon as well as for Bunny Lee. His recordings during the 1980s and early '90s reflected the guns-and-
sex obsession of most ragga music, but with a strong
element of criticism against the evils that drag down
those trapped in poverty: drugs, materialism, and violence. In 1992, Banton was heavily criticized in both
Europe and the United States for his song "Boom
Boom Bye Bye," which was interpreted as advocating

violence against homosexuals. In 1993, after the murder of his friend, Panhead, Banton wrote the song
"Murderer," condemning guns, and began to grow
dreadlocks and move toward more spiritual songs. In
many ways, Banton was
merely the first in a
group of artists in the
1990s who seemed to be
returning to the more
universal concerns seen
earlier in roots reggae,
triggering in some parts
of the world a revival in
the popularity of the
roots reggae not seen
since the heyday of the
Wailers.

Buju Banton

In many ways, the revival of interest in roots reggae was not just a return to the spirituality of the
earlier music, but also an extension of it. Just as
ragga used modern technology to create a hyped-up
dancehall beat, the reggae of today has also taken
advantage of technology, using the best of both
styles of music. Much of the renewed interest in reggae is due to an increased interest in other cultures,
and to Bob Marley's son, Ziggy (David) Marley, and
the Melody Makers (made up of Ziggy's sisters,
Sharon and Cedella Marley, and his brother,

Stephen Marley), who have carried on Bob Marley's work. Throughout the 1990s, Bob Marley's family issued collections of his best music, while Ziggy Marley and the Melody Makers made their own mark in reggae.

Ziggy Marley and the Melody Makers cut their first single, "Children Playing In the Streets," shortly after Bob Marley's death. It was one of the few songs they have recorded that was written by their father, and was later included on their album *Play the Game Right*, issued in 1985. Their 1989 album, *One Bright Day*, garnered greater notice. More original and innovative, in many ways, it marks Ziggy Marley and the Melody Makers' coming into their own. "This album to me sound a little stronger," Ziggy Marley admitted in *Time*. "A little stronger in the beat. It feel harder, with more aggression. I sing it more aggressive. I'm getting older. Music is a weapon. You can use a gun for murder, or you can use it to defend yourself."[15] In the new millennium, Ziggy Marley and the Melody Makers have gone even further in developing a unique and very appealing style of music, luring not only the fans of traditional reggae, but also fans from the ranks of rap music and rock. The group is not alone in bringing reggae back to popularity, however. The popularity of dancehall and reggae artists such as UB40, Shaggy, and Bad Boys, and the Canadian singer Snow, whose hit album *Twelve Inches of Snow* topped U.S. charts in 1993, caused *Billboard* magazine to inaugurate a reggae Top Twenty-five chart.

At the turn of the century, reggae music is still going strong, testament to the universal appeal of its messages and rhythms. While other trends and music come and go, reggae seems to be here to stay—and it has spread around the world. In many countries of Africa, for example, reggae is developing in unique ways that reflect the culture and concerns of their peoples.

9 REGGAE AROUND THE WORLD

Me love all the reggae artists, man, knowing that they don't understand the situation and that them can do better. Me love all of them, cos them 'ave the same feeling as me.

—Bob Marley, NME, 1975[1]

THE YEAR 1999 WAS A SAD ONE FOR REGGAE. IN JULY, the so-called "Crown Prince of Reggae," Dennis Brown, who had earned a Grammy nomination in 1995 for his album *Light My Fire*, died at the age of 42. Later, in December, Joe Higgs passed away. Higgs had mentored a generation or more of great reggae artists, and had himself contributed to the genre with his own songs and music. Despite these melancholy events, however, reggae music was stronger than ever, speaking to people around the world.

On September 18, 1999, two thousand members of the Hopi Tribe gathered at an amphitheater in

Dennis Brown

Kykotomovi, Arizona, to listen to the reggae bands on the Tevi Spirit of Unity tour. Why? "It's most the lyrics," said Jennifer Joseph, who grew up on the Hopi reservation. "They sing about the same things we feel. They sing about oppression, and we feel that here. And they sing about peace and unity in the world, which is what our religion teaches us. But it's the beat, too. It has the same feel as our tribal drumming."[2]

The Hopi not only listen to reggae, they play it. Casper Lomayesva, a Hopi singer, has made a reggae album, *Original Landlord*, on his own label, Third Mesa Records. And the Hopi are not the only Native Americans to see a commonality of experience in the messages of reggae; in the 1990s, Native American John Williams formed an all-Native reggae band.

Around the world, reggae speaks to and for people, and is more popular than ever with its message of peace and love, and its irresistible rhythms. In 1989, the music's popularity was recognized in the United States by the establishment of a reggae category in the annual Grammy Awards.

Because of its large immigrant population from

Jamaica, Great Britain took to reggae from the very beginning. During the 1960s, reggae was the music not only of Jamaican immigrants, but also was adopted by the "skinheads," young white men disaffected by society at the time. Although by the end of that decade, the skinheads had abandoned their allegiance to reggae, the music was firmly entrenched in the United Kingdom because of early Jamaican producers such as Stanley Motta and Coxsone Dodd, and, of course, Britain's own Chris Blackwell. Bob Marley toured extensively in Great Britain during the 1970s, inspiring a huge following as well as many imitators. Recording studios specializing in British reggae sprang up during this period to meet the demand for a home-grown product: Jordan's, Easy Street, Ariwav, Greensleeve, and Fashion Records, among others. The music of the artists being recorded, such as Aswad, Maxi Priest, Tippa Irie, and Phillip Papa Levi, took on a uniquely British flavor. While the more modern forms of reggae—ragga and dancehall—and even the older ska come and go in popularity in Great Britain, roots reggae has never lost its audience. And the same holds true in other countries, particularly in Africa.

In December of 1978, Bob Marley traveled to Ethiopia to visit Rastafarianism's homeland, and in April of 1980, he returned to the continent to per-form in Zimbabwe's Independence Day celebrations. As with the Native Americans, Marley's music and reggae's beat spoke to his audiences and captivated them completely. Two singers in particular have pioneered reggae in Africa: Lucky Dube of South Africa, and Alpha Blondy of Dimbokru; both have achieved international fame.

Lucky Dube was a library assistant in his hometown of Ermelo near Johannesburg, South Africa, when he first became interested in music and joined a band called Skyway. During his work in the library, Dube discovered Rastafarianism, and its music, reggae. He first signed with Gallo records as a mbaqanga singer, singing "the 'zulu jive' style made famous by Paul Simon's 'Graceland.'"[3] Encouraged by the success of a reggae song he had written for his mother, Dube decided to do a reggae album. After seven successful albums in his homeland, he stunned the world with his 1988

Lucky Dube

album, *Slave*, backed by his band, now called The Slaves. By the time his second album, *Together as One*, with its overtly political messages, was released in 1989, South African reggae was recognized as a powerful force in the genre. His messages are those that have driven reggae since its inception:

> It's the message of coming together of the people. Unity is the message. We're not talking unity, say, amongst the black community, we're talking unity amongst everybody. You know? Because we're got to be together as one. God didn't create white men or black men. God just created men in his image. We are his children. There's no reason to be separated like we are.[4]

Another African singer who had risen to international notice is Alpha Blondy (Koné Seydou), of Dimbokru (formerly the Ivory Coast). Growing up in Dimbokru, Blondy heard not the traditional music of Africa, but the rock music popular in the United States at the time. "I grew up listening to Mick Jagger," he says. "That's how I got into reggae music."[5]

Alpha Blondy started playing rock in a high school band. He came to New York to attend college, and began playing reggae. After his return to Dimbokru, he put together a reggae band which then competed on a television talent show that led to his first album,

Jah Glory, on which he was backed by the Natty Rebels, although on his later albums he was usually backed by his touring band, the Solar System. He gained international notice with his 1987 album *Apartheid Is Nazism*. On his albums, Blondy's music usually deals with international political issues, and he incorporates West African rhythms into his music. But, he says, the difference between his music and that of others is "that I would never advise people to go mash it up. I would not encourage violence. I think my music can create the consciousness of a peaceful solution, because I don't believe in a mash-it-up solution."[6] Over the years, Alpha Blondy has worked with the original Wailers' band, which backed his song "Cocody Rock" (1988), and toured the world.

Lucky Dube and Alpha Blondy are only two of the many outstanding reggae artists coming out of Africa. From Mali comes the "Wass-reggae" sound of Askia Modibo that blends "all that is pentatonic: the musics of the Songhai, the Tamachek, Wassoulou, Bambara. . . ."[7] Nigeria contributes Majek Fashek, who boasts of his "pangolo rhythms," while the reggae of Ghana's Rocky Dawuni and his group Local Crisis celebrates freedom and independence.[8] These and many other African artists are carrying on a tradition that was begun when Bob Marley performed in Harare, Zimbabwe, and carrying it on superbly.

Africa is not alone, however, in having taken to

reggae and made the music its own. Around the world, reggae artists are blending their musical traditions with those of reggae to produce a unique music that speaks not only to their countrymen, but to the world. The Australian Aboriginal band, Blekbala Mujik, uses Aboriginal musical instruments such as the didgeridoo to enhance its form of reggae, singing both in English and an Aboriginal language. The band came to international notice playing at the WOMAD international festivals in Spain and in London in 1997. Blekbala Mujik was preceded in Australia by another Aboriginal band, No Fixed Address, their name a reference to the Aboriginal ritual of walkabout. They, too, added a didgeridoo to their music to achieve a Down Under effect.

In France, reggae is alive and well in the music and singing of the band Kreyol Syndikat. "Composed of French Caribbean and West African players now based in Paris, they came together in the early '90s. Their reality-based lyrics deal with social maladies and positive themes sung in French creole."[9] In Wales, the Welsh band Llwybr Llaethog which formed in 1985 released a dub album, *Mewn Dyb (In Dub)*, in 1996. Nicaragua has the reggae band Soul Vibrations, whose "Soul Vibrations" protested the electoral victory of President Violeta Chamorro over the Sandinistas. And Brazil swings to the music of Zeca Baleiro (José de Ribamar

Coelho Santos) who combines the rhythms of samba with those of reggae. In Japan, female vocalist Sayoko adapted a pop Japanese tune in a CD single, "Ue O Muite Aruko," adding reggae beats.

Around the world, reggae rhythms throb, but there is more to reggae than just the beat. The basic messages of peace and love that the original reggae artists intended the music to convey also travel with the music's rhythms, as do the ideals of black pride and racial awareness that were inherent not only in reggae but in Rastafarianism. They have captured black audiences around the world, and are also influencing white audiences and musicians. The music has, as critic Chris Potash says, a "double-edged beauty . . . food for thought, a beat that moves bodies."[10] On the Internet, there are thousands of Web sites from countries around the world and in all the languages of the world celebrating reggae. Behind many advertisements on television and on the radio, there are often the enticing rhythms of reggae luring consumers to buy. Movie sound tracks bounce with an island beat. Reggae has infiltrated every corner of our existence. Reggae is no longer merely the music of the island of Jamaica. Around the world, reggae rules.

The Jamaican national motto is "Out of Many, One People," and the music that originated on that tiny

Caribbean island seems to be doing a great deal to extend that motto to the entire world. The music that began so long ago with the rhythms of the burru drums of Africa mixed with swaying mento beats has spread throughout the world, uniting musicians and fans in a commonality of experience, something those who began it and first popularized it never imagined. It was an impossible dream that came true. As Bob Marley said, "I'll tell ya somet'ing, mon, me never t'ought reggae gon' become popular over da world, reachin' many ears, when it was beginnin'."[11]

ENDNOTES

1 SWEET JAMAICA

1. As quoted in Taylor, Don. *Marley and Me: The Real Bob Marley Story*. New York: Barricade Books, 1995: 15.
2. Cohen, Steve. *Adventure Guide to Jamaica*, 3rd ed. Edison, N.J.: Hunter Publishing, Inc., 1997: 3.
3. Wilson, Annie. *Essential Jamaica*. Lincolnwood, Ill.: Passport Books, 1996: 12.
4. Ibid., 14.
5. Dolan, Sean. *Bob Marley*. Philadelphia: Chelsea House Publishing, 1997: 22.
6. Cohen: 8.
7. As quoted in Nicholls, Kristin. "Jamaican Artists and Producers" in *The Dread Library*. http://debate.uvm.edu/dreadlibrary/nicholls.html; accessed: 2/2/00.

2 MARCUS GARVEY AND RASTAFARIANISM

1. As quoted in Taylor, op. cit.: 136.
2. Wilson, op. cit.: 16.
3. Davis, Stephen, and Peter Simon, as quoted in Winders, James A. "From Reggae, Rastafarians and Revolution: Rock Music in the Third World," in *Reggae, Rasta, Revolution: Jamaican Music From Ska to Dub*, Chris Potash, ed. New York: Schirmer Books, Simon & Schuster-Macmillan, 1997: 18.
4. As quoted in Taylor: 240.
5. Barrow, Steve, and Peter Dalton. *Reggae, The Rough Guide*. London: The Rough Guides, Ltd., 1997: 136.
6. "Marcus Garvey." *The New Grolier Multimedia Encyclopedia*. Novato, Calif.: Software Toolworks, Inc./ Grolier, Inc., 1993.
7. Ibid.
8. Winders: 16.
9. "Rastafarianism." Arrayed Roots Sounds: Rastafarian Cultural Page. http://www.geocities.c...Strip/Amphitheatre/2639/ARSCul.html; accessed: 5/10/99.
10. Wilson: 17.
11. Winders: 15.
12. Ibid.: 18.
13. Ibid.: 17–18.
14. Taylor: 247.
15. bid.: 248.
16. Winders: 18.
17. Barrow and Dalton: 136.
18. Winders: 16.
19. Larkin, Colin. *The Virgin Encyclopedia of Reggae*. London: Virgin Books, 1998: 241.
20. Taylor: 250–251.

3 SOUNDS OUT OF AFRICA

1. Reckord, Verena. "Reggae, Rastafarianism and Cultural Identity," in Potash, op. cit.: 3–4.
2. Ibid.: 4.
3. White, Timothy. *Catch a Fire: The Life of Bob Marley.* New York: Henry Holt & Co., 1998: 136.
4. Barrow and Dalton, op. cit.: 162, 376.
5. Davis, James D. "Children of the Ras," in Potash, op. cit.: 254.
6. Bender, Wolfgang. *Sweet Mothers.* Chicago, Ill.: University of Chicago Press, 1991: 17–18.
7. Barrow and Dalton: 5.
8. Ibid.: 6.
9. Shirley-Henry, Sharon. "The History of Jamaica's Music," in *Jamaica's Musical History.* 1999; jamaicadancehall.com. http://www.jamaicadancehall.com/musichistory.html; accessed: 2/12/00.
10. "Barbados Music: Calypso." *Discover Barbados!* http://www.divefree.net/music/calypso.htm; accessed: 2/12/00.
11. White: 17.
12. Reckord: 5.
13. Nicholls, op. cit.
14. White: 17.
15. Barrow and Dalton: 7.

4 BIG SOUNDS, BIG SYSTEMS

1. Bradley, Lloyd. "Introduction" to *Reggae on CD,* in Potash, op. cit.: 105.
2. Barrow and Dalton, op. cit.: 11.
3. Nicholls, op. cit.
4. Barrow and Dalton: 11.
5. As quoted in Nicholls: 3.
6. Barrow and Dalton: 16.
7. Larkin, op. cit.: 227.
8. Barrow and Dalton: 19.
9. Rhodes, Henry A. "The Evolution of Rap Music in the United States." *Yale-New Haven Teachers Institute,* 1998. http://www.cis.yale.edu/ynhti/curriculum/units/1993/4/93.04.04.x.html#a; accessed: 24 March 1999.
10. White, op. cit.: 18.
11. Larkin: 86.
12. Ibid.: 81.
13. Ibid.: 227.
14. Davis, Stephen, and Peter Simon. *Reggae Bloodlines: In Search of the Music and Culture of Jamaica.* New York: Da Capo Press, Inc., 1992: 12.
15. Larkin: 30.
16. White: 18.

5 JAMAICAN BEATS: SKA AND ROCK STEADY

1. Cocks, Jay. "The Ska Above, the Beat Below," in Potash, op. cit.: 131.

2. Larkin, op. cit.: 273.

3. Foster, op. cit.: 9.

4. Gonzalez, Fernando. "Reunited Jamaican Group Marks Year's End in Style." in Potash, op. cit.: 134.

5. Ibid.

6. Ibid.: 19.

7. Ibid.: 103.

8. Barrow and Dalton, op. cit.: 51.

9. White, op. cit. 20.

10. Barrow and Dalton: 24.

11. *Burnin' Vernon's Original Ska Page.* http://equinox.unr.edu/homepage/lvb/; accessed: 2/6/00: 2.

12. White: 155.

6 BOB MARLEY AND THE BIRTH OF ROOTS REGGAE

1. As quoted in Bennett, Scotty. *Bob Marley.* New York: St. Martin's Press: 27.

2. Ibid.: 30.

3. White, op. cit.: 152–153.

4. Barrow and Dalton, op. cit.: 83.

5. As quoted in Dolan, op. cit.: 79.

6. As quoted in Bennett: 29.

7. Ibid.: 18.

8. As quoted in "Peter Tosh" in Chris Salewicz, *BobMarley.Com: The Wailers.* 1995. http://www.bobmarley.com/life/wailers/tosh.html; accessed: 2/12/00.

9. Taylor, op. cit.: 141.

10. As quoted in Bennet: 75.

11. Ibid.: 76.

12. As quoted in Dolan: 113.

7 BEYOND THE WAILERS

1. As quoted in Bennett, op. cit: 54.

2. Larkin, op. cit.:187.

3. Barrow and Dalton, op. cit.: 37.

4. Bangs, Lester. "How to Learn to Love Reggae," in Potash, op. cit.: 78–79.

5. *Rolling Stone.* "Jimmy Cliff: Paving the Way for Reggae," in Potash, op. cit.: 85.

6. Larkin: 62.

7. *Rolling Stone:* 86.

8. Larkin: 221.

9. Ibid.: 223.

10. Jones, Simon. From "Black Culture, White Youth: The Reggae Tradition From JA to UK" (1988); MacMillan Education Ltd. *Reggae Features*. http://www.easystar.com/feature2.html; accessed: 5/10/99.

11. White, op. cit.: 152, 497.

12. Ibid.

8 NEW WAVES IN JAMAICA: DUB, DANCEHALL, AND RAGGA

1. Toop, David. From *Ocean of Sound: Aether Talk, Ambient Sound and Imaginary Worlds*, in Potash, op. cit.: 152.

2. "A Brief History of Dub." *History of Dub Music*. http://www.geocities.com/EnchantedForest/Meadow/8887/; accessed 12/3/99.

3. Barrow, Steve. As quoted in Dub Gone Crazy. http://www.interruptor.ch/dub.html; accessed: 10/17/99.

4. As quoted in Barrow and Dalton, op. cit.: 203.

5. "A Brief History of Dub."

6. Weidenbaum, Marc. "Dub, American Style" in Potash, op. cit.: 180.

7. Ibid.: 184.

8. Larkin, op. cit.: 72, 73.

9. Barrow and Dalton: 231.

10. Garcia, Guy, with reporting by David E. Thigpen. "Marley's Ghost." *Time*. 13 Sept. 1993, in *Time Almanac: Reference Edition*. CD-Rom. Fort Lauderdale, Fla.: Time Inc. Magazine Co. and Compact Publishing, Inc., 1994.

11. Thielen, Ben. "The Change of Messages in Dancehall." *The Dread Library*. http://debate.uvm.edu/dreadlibrary/thielen.html: accessed: 5/12/00.

12. As quoted in Thielen: 4.

13. Larkin: 235.

14. As quoted in Thielen: 6.

15. "New Directions for The Next Decade." *Time*. 4 Sept. 1989; 13 Sept. 1993, in *Time Almanac: Reference Edition*.

9 REGGAE AROUND THE WORLD

1. As quoted in Bennett, Scotty, op. cit.: 54.

2. Weber, Bruce. "Reggae Rhythms Speak to an Insular Tribe." *New York Times*, 19 Sept. 1999: 36.

3. Putumayo World Music. *Reggae Around the World*. http://putumayo.com/ed/regwld/regwld.html; accessed: 6/8/99.

4. As quoted in Foster, op. cit.:140.

5. As quoted in Foster: 133.

6. As quoted in Potash, "Alpha Blondy's Message is Dead Serious," in Potash, op. cit.: 243.

7. Putumayo World Music: 4.

8. Ibid.: 4, 6.

9. Ibid.: 5.

10. Potash, "Introduction" in Potash, op. cit.: xxi.

11. As quoted in Potash: xxviii.

"Barbados Music: Calypso." *Discover Barbados!* http://www.divefree.net/music/calypso.htm; accessed: 2/12/00.

Barrett, Leonard. *The Rastafarians.* Boston: South End Press, 1997.

Barrow, Steve, and Peter Dalton. *Reggae, The Rough Guide.* London: The Rough Guides Ltd., 1997.

Bender, Wolfgang. *Sweet Mothers.* Chicago, Ill.: University of Chicago Press, 1991.

Bennett, Scotty. *Bob Marley.* New York: St. Martin's Press, 1997.

"A Brief History of Dub." *History of Dub Music.* http://www.geocities.com/EnchantedForest/Meadow/8887/; accessed: 12/3/99.

Burnin' Vernon's Original Ska Page. http://equinox.unr.edu/homepage/lvb/; accessed: 2/6/00.

"Calypso." *The New Grolier Multimedia Encyclopedia.* Novato, Calif.: Software Toolworks, Inc.–Grolier, Inc., 1993.

Campbell, Horace. *Rasta and Resistance: From Marcus Garvey to Walter Rodney.* Trenton, N.J.: Africa World Press, 1987.

Chang, Kevin O'Brien, and Wayne Chen. *Reggae Routes: The Story of Jamaican Music.* Philadelphia: Temple University Press, 2000.

Cohen, Steve. *Adventure Guide to Jamaica,* 3rd ed. Edison, N.J.: Hunter Publishing, Inc., 1997.

Davis, Stephen, and Peter Simon. *Reggae Bloodlines: In Search of the Music and Culture of Jamaica.* New York: Da Capo Press, Inc., 1992.

Dolan, Sean. *Bob Marley.* Philadelphia, Penn.: Chelsea House Publishing, 1997.

Dub Gone Crazy. http://www.interruptor.ch/dub.html; accessed: 10/17/99.

Foster, Chuck. *Roots, Rock, Reggae: An Oral History of Reggae Music from Ska to Dancehall.* New York: Billboard Books, Watson-Guptill Publications, 1999.

Garcia, Guy, with reporting by David E. Thigpen. "Marley's Ghost." *Time*. 13 Sept. 1993. *Time Almanac: Reference Edition*. CD-ROM. Fort Lauderdale, Fla.: Time Inc. Magazine Co. & Compact Publishing, Inc., 1994.

"The History of Jamaica." *All-Inclusive: The Jamaica Experts*. 1994–2000, All-Inclusive Vacations. http://www.all-inclusive.com/jam2.html; accessed: 1/3/00.

"History of Jamaican People." *People and History of Jamaica*. http://www.ktis.net/~rpmusgra/jamhist.htm; accessed: 1/11/00.

"Information About Jamaica." Ibis Too Co. Ltd.– *fantasyisle.com*. 1999. http://www.fantasyisle.com/history.htm; accessed: 1/11/00.

Jahn, Brian, and Tom Weber. *Reggae Island: Jamaican Music in the Digital Age*. Kingston, Jamaica: Kingston Publishers, 1992.

"JamaicanMarketPlace—A Quality Experience." *History of Jamaica*. wysiwyg://34/http://www.jamaicamarketplace.com/history.htm; accessed: 1/11/00.

"Jamaica's Reggae Music." *ReggaeFusionJamiaca*. Don-Getz Limited, 1999. http://www.reggaefusion.com/Evolution/Reggae.html; accessed: 3/22/00.

Jones, Simon. From *Black Culture, White Youth: The Reggae Tradition from JA to UK*. MacMillan Education Ltd., 1988.

"Junior Braithwaite." *San Francisco Chronicle*. 2000. http://www.afgate.com/cgibin.article.cgi?file=/chronicle/archive/1999/06/05/MN92075.DTL; accessed: 7/12/00.

"The Land of Jamaica." *All-Inclusive: The Jamaica Experts*. 1994–2000, All-Inclusive Vacations. http://www.all-inclusive.com/jam1.html; accessed: 1/3/00.

Larkin, Colin. *The Virgin Encyclopedia of Reggae*. London: Virgin Books, 1998.

"Marcus Garvey." *The New Grolier Multimedia Encyclopedia*. Novato, Calif.: Software Toolworks, Inc./Grolier, Inc., 1993.

"Marcus Garvey." *Time Almanac: Reference Edition*. CD-ROM. Fort Lauderdale, Fla.:
Time Inc. Magazine Co. & Compact Publishing, Inc., 1994.

Marley, Rita. *Bob Marley: Songs of Freedom*. New York: Penguin Books, 1995.

McCormack, Ed. "Bob Marley With a Bullet." *Rolling Stone*. 12 August 1976, 34.

"New Directions for the Next Decade." *Time*. 4 Sept. 1989; 13 Sept. 1993.
Time Almanac: Reference Edition. CD-ROM. Fort Lauderdale, Fla.: Time Inc. Magazine Co.
and Compact Publishing, Inc., 1994.

Nicholas, Tracy, and Bill Sparrow. *Rastafari: A Way of Life*. Chicago: Frontline Distribution
International, 1996.

Nicholls, Kristin. "Jamaican Artists and Producers." *The Dread Library*.
http://debate.uvm.edu/dreadlibrary/nicholls.html; accessed: 2/2/00.

"Original Wailer Junior Braithwaite Murdered in Jamaica." *Junior Braithwaite Page* in *Fuller Up,
The Dead Musician Directory*. http://www.elvispelvis.com/juniorbraithwaite.htm#bio;
accessed: 7/12/00.

Pawka, Mike. *Rasta/Patois Dictionary*. http://niceup.com/patois.txt; accessed: 6/8/99.

Potash, Chris, ed., *Reggae, Rasta, Revolution: Jamaican Music from Ska to Dub*. New York:
Schirmer Books, 1997.

Putumayo World Music. *Reggae Around the World*. http://putumayo.com/ed/regwld/regwld.html;
accessed: 6/8/99.

"Rastafari in Jamaica." *About Rastafari: Bob Marley School for the Arts Institute*. 1999.
http://www.bobartsinstitute.edu/Rastafari.htm; accessed: 1/3/00.

"Rastafarianism." *Arrayed Roots Sounds: Rastafarian Cultural Page*.
http://www.geocities.c...Strip/Amphitheatre/2639/ARSCul.html; accessed: 5/10/99.

Reggae Features. http://www.easystar.com/feature2.html; accessed: 5/10/99.

Reggae History. http://www.webbnet.com/~Mandolin/history.html; accessed: 3/22/00.

Rhodes, Henry A. "The Evolution of Rap Music in the United States." *Yale-New Haven Teachers Institute*, 1998. http://www.cis.yale.edu/ynhti/curriculum/units/1993/4/93.04.04.x.html#a; accessed: 24 March 1999.

Rosenthal, Brian. "The History of Ska!!!" *Arrayed Roots Sounds*. http://www.geocities.c...StripAmphitheatre/2639/ARSSka.html; accessed: 5/10/99.

Salewicz, Chris. "Peter Tosh." *BobMarley.Com*. 1995. http://www.bobmarley.com/life/wailers/tosh.html; accessed: 2/12/00.

Shirley-Henry, Sharon. "The History of Jamaica's Music." *Jamaica's Music History*. 1999. http://www.jamaicadancehall.com/musichistory.html; accessed: 2/12/00.

Taylor, Don. *Marley and Me: The Real Bob Marley Story*. New York: Barricade Books, Inc., 1995.

Thielen, Ben. "The Change of Messages in Dancehall." *The Dread Library*. http://debate.uvm.edu/dreadlibrary/thielen.html; accessed: 5/12/00.

Thurnton, Hayes Kali. "Rasta Roots Run Deep in Resistance." *Montreal Community Contact*, November 1998, p. 71. http://debate.uvm.edu/thurnton11-98.html; accessed: 5/10/99.

Wadsworth, Alison. "Jazz and Blues Feedback to Jamaica." *The Dread Library*. http://debate.uvm.edu/dreadlibrary/wadsworth.html; accessed: 4/23/00.

Weber, Bruce. "Reggae Rhythms Speak to an Insular Tribe." *New York Times*, 19 Sept. 1999: 1, 36.

White, Timothy. *Catch a Fire: The Life of Bob Marley*. New York: Henry Holt & Co., 1998.

Wilson, Annie. *Essential Jamaica*. Lincolnwood, Ill.: Passport Books, 1996.

page ii   Delroy Wilson: © David Corio / MICHAEL OCHS ARCHIVES, Venice, Calif.

page vi   Bob Marley: © Chuck Krall / MICHAEL OCHS ARCHIVES, Venice, Calif.

page 9   Workers on a Jamaican plantation: © Corbis, Inc., Bellevue, Wash.

page 20   Marcus Garvey: © Corbis, Inc., Bellevue, Wash.

page 23   Haile Selassie: © Corbis, Inc., Bellevue, Wash.

page 24   Haile Selassie and the royal family: © Corbis, Inc., Bellevue, Wash.

page 37   Quadrille dance: photo provided by the Jamaica Information Services, Jamaica.

page 41   Mento band: photo provided by the Jamaica Information Services, Jamaica.

page 43   Harry Belafonte: © MICHAEL OCHS ARCHIVES, Venice, Calif.

page 51   Lee Perry: © David Corio / © MICHAEL OCHS ARCHIVES, Venice, Calif.

page 60   Millie Small: © David Redfern / REDFERNS, London, U.K.

page 64   Delroy Wilson: © David Corio / MICHAEL OCHS ARCHIVES, Venice, Calif.

page 68   Bob Marley: © Chuck Krall / MICHAEL OCHS ARCHIVES, Venice, Calif.

page 74   Bunny Wailer: © John Kirk / REDFERNS, London, U.K.

page 76   Bob Marley and the Wailers: © MICHAEL OCHS ARCHIVES, Venice, Calif.

page 80   Rita Marley: © MICHAEL OCHS ARCHIVES, Venice, Calif.

page 83   Peter Tosh: © Chuck Krall / MICHAEL OCHS ARCHIVES, Venice, Calif.

page 89   Bob Marley with I-Three: © MICHAEL OCHS ARCHIVES, Venice, Calif.

page 92   Ziggy Marley: © Al Pereira / MICHAEL OCHS ARCHIVES, Venice, Calif.

page 97   Jimmy Cliff: © Jan Jenson / MICHAEL OCHS ARCHIVES, Venice, Calif.

page 113   Yellowman : © Lisa Haun / MICHAEL OCHS ARCHIVES, Venice, Calif.

page 114   Buju Banton: © Des Willie / REDFERNS, London, U.K.

page 118   Dennis Brown: © David Corio / MICHAEL OCHS ARCHIVES, Venice, Calif.

page 119   Lucky Dube: © David Redfern / REDFERNS, London, U.K.

INDEX

Page numbers in italics refer to pages with illustrations.